Trust in Social Media

Synthesis Lectures on Information Security, Privacy, & Trust

Editors
Elisa Bertino, *Purdue University*
Ravi Sandhu, *University of Texas, San Antonio*

The Synthesis Lectures Series on Information Security, Privacy, and Trust publishes 50- to 100-page publications on topics pertaining to all aspects of the theory and practice of Information Security, Privacy, and Trust. The scope largely follows the purview of premier computer security research journals such as ACM Transactions on Information and System Security, IEEE Transactions on Dependable and Secure Computing and Journal of Cryptology, and premier research conferences, such as ACM CCS, ACM SACMAT, ACM AsiaCCS, ACM CODASPY, IEEE Security and Privacy, IEEE Computer Security Foundations, ACSAC, ESORICS, Crypto, EuroCrypt and AsiaCrypt. In addition to the research topics typically covered in such journals and conferences, the series also solicits lectures on legal, policy, social, business, and economic issues addressed to a technical audience of scientists and engineers. Lectures on significant industry developments by leading practitioners are also solicited.

Mobile Platform Security
N. Asokan, Lucas Davi, Alexandra Dmitrienko, Stephan Heuser, Kari Kostiainen, Elena Reshetova, and Ahmad-Reza Sadeghi
2013

Security and Trust in Online Social Networks
Barbara Carminati, Elena Ferrari, and Marco Viviani
2013

RFID Security and Privacy
Yingjiu Li, Robert H. Deng, and Elisa Bertino
2013

Hardware Malware
Christian Krieg, Adrian Dabrowski, Heidelinde Hobel, Katharina Krombholz, and Edgar Weippl
2013

Private Information Retrieval
Xun Yi, Russell Paulet, and Elisa Bertino
2013

Privacy for Location-based Services
Gabriel Ghinita
2013

Enhancing Information Security and Privacy by Combining Biometrics with Cryptography
Sanjay G. Kanade, Dijana Petrovska-Delacrétaz, and Bernadette Dorizzi
2012

Analysis Techniques for Information Security
Anupam Datta, Somesh Jha, Ninghui Li, David Melski, and Thomas Reps
2010

Operating System Security
Trent Jaeger
2008

Trust in Social Media
Jiliang Tang and Huan Liu

ISBN: 978-3-031-01217-4 paperback
ISBN: 978-3-031-02345-3 ebook

DOI 10.1007/978-3-031-02345-3

A Publication in the Springer series
SYNTHESIS LECTURES ON INFORMATION SECURITY, PRIVACY, & TRUST

Lecture #13
Series Editors: Elisa Bertino, *Purdue University*
     Ravi Sandhu, *University of Texas, San Antonio*
Series ISSN
Print 1945-9742 Electronic 1945-9750

Trust in Social Media

Jiliang Tang and Huan Liu
Arizona State University

SYNTHESIS LECTURES ON INFORMATION SECURITY, PRIVACY, & *TRUST #13*

ABSTRACT

Social media greatly enables people to participate in online activities and shatters the barrier for online users to create and share information at any place at any time. However, the explosion of user-generated content poses novel challenges for online users to find relevant information, or, in other words, exacerbates the information overload problem. On the other hand, the quality of user-generated content can vary dramatically from excellence to abuse or spam, resulting in a problem of information credibility. The study and understanding of trust can lead to an effective approach to addressing both information overload and credibility problems.

Trust refers to a relationship between a trustor (the subject that trusts a target entity) and a trustee (the entity that is trusted). In the context of social media, trust provides evidence about with whom we can trust to share information and from whom we can accept information without additional verification. With trust, we make the mental shortcut by directly seeking information from trustees or trusted entities, which serves a two-fold purpose: without being overwhelmed by excessive information (i.e., mitigated information overload) and with credible information due to the trust placed on the information provider (i.e., increased information credibility). Therefore, trust is crucial in helping social media users collect relevant and reliable information, and trust in social media is a research topic of increasing importance and of practical significance. This book takes a computational perspective to offer an overview of characteristics and elements of trust and illuminate a wide range of computational tasks of trust. It introduces basic concepts, deliberates challenges and opportunities, reviews state-of-the-art algorithms, and elaborates effective evaluation methods in the trust study. In particular, we illustrate properties and representation models of trust, elucidate trust prediction with representative algorithms, and demonstrate real-world applications where trust is explicitly used. As a new dimension of the trust study, we discuss the concept of distrust and its roles in trust computing.

KEYWORDS

trust in social media, representing trust, predicting trust, applying trust, incorporating distrust

To my parents and wife Hui.

–JT

To my parents, wife, and sons.

–HL

Contents

Acknowledgments

First and foremost, we are thankful to our colleagues at the Data Mining and Machine Learning Lab for their helpful suggestions: Xufei Wang, Huiji Gao, Xia Hu, Pritam Gundecha, Fred Morstatter, Shamanth Kumar, Ali Abbasi, Reza Zafarani, Rob Trevino, Isaac Jones, Geoffery Barbier, Salem Alelyani, Zhuo Feng, Tahora H. Nazer, Suhang Wang, Suhas Ranganath, Jundong Li, Liang Wu, Ghazaleh Beigi, and Kewei Cheng.

We would like to acknowledge Morgan & Claypool, particularly the Executive Editor Diane D. Cerra for her patience, help, and encouragement throughout this project. This work is part of the projects sponsored by grants from the National Science Foundation (NSF) under grant number IIS-1217466, the U.S. Army Research Office (ARO) under contract/grant number 025071, the Office of Naval Research(ONR) under grant number N000141010091, and a research fund from Yahoo Faculty Research and Engagement Program.

Last but not the least, we are deeply indebted to our families for their support through this entire project. We dedicate this book to them, with love.

Jiliang Tang and Huan Liu
August 2015

CHAPTER 1

Introduction

Social media greatly enables people to participate in online activities such as networking, sharing, tagging, and commenting. A recent survey about social media activities shows that the top activity is reading posts and viewing pictures, followed by playing games, updating profiles, and commenting and posting.[1] The popularity of social media shatters the barrier for online users to create and share information at any place at any time. User-generated content accumulates at an unprecedented rate. For example, 500 million tweets are tweeted on Twitter[2] per day and more than 40 million photos are uploaded to Instagram.[3] Given the big data problem, it becomes difficult for social media users to find relevant information, or, in other words, exacerbates the *information overload* problem. How can we find relevant content? Anyone can publish content in social media and with so many grass-roots authors, from whom we should collect information relevant to us? On the other hand, the quality of user generated content varies widely from excellent to abusive or spamming, resulting in a problem of *information credibility*. For example, more than 40% of tweets are pointless babble. How to find reliable information fast? Since anyone in social media may access our content, with whom should we share information? The study and understanding of trust can lead to an effective approach to addressing aforementioned information overload and credibility problems.

Trust refers to a relationship between a trustor (the subject that trusts a target entity) and a trustee (the entity that is trusted) [5, 95], as shown in Figure 1.1. In the context of social media, trust helps answer questions such as with whom we can trust to share information and from whom we can accept information without additional verification. With trust, we make the mental shortcut by directly seeking information from trustees or trusted entities, which serves a two-fold purpose: without being overwhelmed by excessive information (i.e., mitigated information overload) and with credible information due to the trust placed on the information provider (i.e., increased information credibility). Therefore, trust is crucial in helping social media users collect relevant and reliable information, and trust in social media is a research topic of increasing importance and of practical significance [38, 62, 139]. We start this chapter with the definitions of trust.

---

[1]http://www.marketingprofs.com/charts/2010/4101/social-media-brand-followers-hunting-for-deals
[2]https://twitter.com/
[3]https://instagram.com/

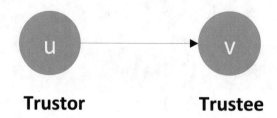

Figure 1.1: Definitions of Trustor and Trustee.

1.1 DEFINITIONS OF TRUST

Trust is a broad and complex concept and it has been investigated extensively by multiple disciplines such as psychology, sociology, economics, management, and computational sciences [100]. Each discipline has its own perspective of trust hence there is still no consensus on definitions of trust and has investigated one part of the trust elephant's anatomy based on its own lens [80]. In the following subsections, we introduce representative definitions in each discipline.

1.1.1   TRUST IN PSYCHOLOGY

In psychology, a person's dispositional tendency to trust others can be considered a personality trait. For example, the higher trusting people are less likely to be conflicted, unhappy, or maladjusted, liked more, less gullible, and sought out as a friend more often, both by low-trusting and high-trusting others [116]. psychologists have mainly analyzed the personality side of trust. One popular definition about trust in psychology is given by Morton Deutch [30]:

- if an individual is confronted with an ambiguous path, a path that can lead to an event perceived to be beneficial (A+) or to an event perceived to be harmful (A-);

- a user perceives that the occurrence of A+ or A- is contingent on the behavior of another person; and

- s/he perceives that strength of A- to be greater than that strength of A+. If s/he chooses to take an ambiguous with such properties, he/she makes a trusting choice.

Another popular definition in psychology is given by Schlenker et al. [120] where trust is defined as "a reliance upon information received from another person about uncertain environmental states and their accompanying outcomes in a risky situation."

1.1.2   TRUST IN SOCIOLOGY

Sociologists have mainly concerned about the position and role of trust in social systems. In sociology, trust is usually defined as a set of expectations shared by all those involved in an exchange [172]. Three expectations of trust are defined in [8] as:

- expectation of the persistence and fulfillment of the natural and moral social orders;

- expectation of "technically competent role performance" from those we interact with in social relationships and systems; and

- expectation that partners in interaction will "carry out their fiduciary obligations and responsibilities, that is, their duties in certain situations to place others' interests before their own."

In addition, Lewis and Weigert define trust as the undertaking of a risky course of action on the confident expectation that all persons involved in the action will act competently and dutifully [81].

1.1.3   TRUST IN ECONOMICS

Trust in economics is used to explain a difference between actual human behavior and the one we desire to maximize one's utility or a difference between Nash equilibrium and the observed equilibrium [104]. Therefore, economists have investigated the rational choice perspective of trust. For example, trust has been extensively studied by economists in game theoretic settings [73] such as social dilemma games, public good games, and trust games and specifically games based on the Prisoner's Dilemma, which are widely used to connect trust with economic utility and demonstrate the rationality behind reciprocity. Below are two representative trust definitions in economics.

Trust is defined as a confidence respecting property reposed in one person (or the trustee), for the benefit of another (or the trustor) and it is measured by how much credit to offer me [71]. In [85], trust is defined as the judgment one makes on the basis of one's past interactions with others that they will seek to act in ways that favor one's interests, rather than harm them, in circumstances that remain to be defined.

1.1.4   TRUST IN MANAGEMENT

Trust in management indicates employee faith in an organization's goal attainment and organizational leaders, and the belief that organizational action will be beneficial for employees [75] and it can influence various organizational phenomena such as job satisfaction, stress, organizational commitment, productivity, and knowledge sharing. For example, trust in management increases overall knowledge exchange while reduces the cost of knowledge exchanges. Therefore, trust in management is usually investigated under the organizational context and following are two popular definitions about trust in management.

Trust is the willingness of a party to be vulnerable to the actions of another part based on the expectation that the other will perform a particular action important to the trustor [99]. Trust is the reliance by one person, group, or firm upon a voluntarily accepted duty on the part of another person, group, or firm to recognize and protect the rights and interests of all others engaged in a joint endeavor or economic exchange [53].

Table 1.1: An interdisciplinary table about definitions of trust. Note that "other characteristics" include attributes like openness and carefulness; "other referent" refers to either people or institutions and values in the table correspond to the number of definitions of trust

Trustee Characteristic or Referent	Conceptual Types					
	Disposition	Structural	Affect or Attitude	Belief or Expectancy	Intention	Behavior
Competence			1	19		4
Benevolence			11	26	3	5
Integrity			9	18	1	6
Predictability			1	11		1
Other Characteristic				7		1
Other Referent	5	6	7	21	5	14

1.1.5   AN INTERDISCIPLINARY VIEW OF TRUST DEFINITIONS

In [100], McKnight and Chervany investigated 65 cited articles and monographs that provided definitions of trust including 23 from the psychology domain, 23 from management, and 19 spread across sociology or economics. They found though different disciplines study trust from different perspectives, trust definitions could be categorized by trust referent, which is typically the characteristics of the trustee, including competence, benevolence, integrity, and predictability. Meanwhile those definitions could also be categorized by conceptual type including disposition, institutional/structural, attitude, belief, expectancy, intention, and behavior. Based on their findings, they provided an interdisciplinary table about definitions of trust as shown in Table 1.1 where the "other characteristics" row includes attributes like openness and carefulness and "other referent" refers to either people or institutions. Note that values in the table correspond to the number of definitions of trust.

1.1.6   DISCUSSIONS

Recently, trust has attracted increasing attention from data science community and data scientists have studied trust mainly from the computational perspective. Many researchers also tried to define trust from the computational perspective. For example, trust is defined as a subjective expectation an agent has about another's future behavior based on the history of their encounters [105], or the explicit opinion expressed by a user about another user regarding the perceived quality of a certain characteristic of this user [95]. The vast majority of those definitions share two common characteristics. One is that the defined trust is inter-personal trust, as shown in Figure 1.1. It refers to a relationship from a user (or a trustor) to another user (or a trustee).

The other is that trust among users can be represented in the form of trust networks. In a trust network, nodes are users, links between users indicate the existences of trust relations, and link weights denote trust values. The focus of this book is interpersonal trust relations, which can be represented as trust networks.

1.2   EXAMPLES OF ONLINE TRUST SYSTEMS

Trust mechanisms have been widely implemented in social media and different social media sites use trust to fulfill different goals. Some aim to increase the number of auctions and online purchase transactions such as eBay and Amazon; some make use of trust to identify experts such as Advogato and AskMe; some want to promote the sale of good products such as Epinions and Ciao; while others take advantage of trust among social media users to improve user engagement and enhance their services such as news sites [62, 95]. Those websites can be categorized into few different types based on their common features and properties as follows [95]:

- e-commerce sites;

- expert sites;

- review sites; and

- new sites.

1.2.1   E-COMMERCE SITES

E-commerce sites are online systems where users can sell and buy items such as eBay,[4] Taobao,[5] and Amazon.[6] In those sites, typically sellers and buyers do not know each other; therefore, there is an issue of trust. Trust in e-commerce sites provide a natural, simple, but reliable way to figure out possible trustworthy commercial partners. Next, we use eBay as an example to illustrate how trust works on e-commerce sites.

eBay is one of the most popular auction sites where sellers are allowed to list items for sale and buyers can bid those items. After transactions between sellers and buyers, both of them can rate each other as positive, negative or neutral. They also can leave comments including positive comments such as "Smooth transaction" and "Thank you!" as well as negative ones such as "Buyers beware!". eBay determines trustworthy scores of users based on those ratings, which is simply calculated as the sum of positive ratings (from unique users) minus the sum of negative ratings (from unique users). Those trustworthy scores provide evidence for both sellers and buyers to help make future decisions.

[4]http://www.ebay.com/
[5]http://www.taobao.com/
[6]http://www.amazon.com/

1.2.2   EXPERT SITES

Expert sites provide platforms for users to seek professional and credible answers to their questions online. Users can rate experts based on the quality of their replies from various perspectives such as correctness, clarity, reliability, and timeliness. Expert sites can identify a pool of individuals to answer questions in their areas of expertise and examples of those sites including AllExperts,[7] AskMe,[8] and Advogato.[9] Next, we demonstrate trust in expert sites via Advogato.

Advogato is a community site of open-source developers. It provides Advogato's trust scheme based on a flow model and users adopt this scheme to rank each other according to how skilled they perceive each other to be. The trust flow starts from the creator of Advogato, Raph Levien, and propagates across the network with a decay factor at each hop. Users can refer others with the following statuses—Apprentice (lowest), Journeyer (medium), or Master (highest). A separate flow graph is computed for each status level and the trustworthy level of a user is the highest one for which there is a flow reaching him/her. For example, if both flow graphs of Master and Apprentice reach a user, he/she will have Master status; while if only the flow graph of Apprentice reaches him/her, the user will have only Apprentice status.

1.2.3   REVIEW SITES

Review sites such as Epinions[10] and Ciao[11] allow their users or may employ professional reviewers to author reviews about businesses, products, or services. It implements trust mechanisms to provide information for consumers for the purpose of making better purchase decisions. Epinions is one of the earliest review sites.

Epinions founded in 1999 is a product review site and its users can write reviews about products, which consists of textual reviews and rating scores from 1–5 stars. Other Epinions users can rate reviews as Not Helpful, Somewhat Helpful, Helpful, and Very Helpful, which is used to determine the helpfulness of the reviews as well as to indicate the statuses of the reviewers. It also provides a trust scheme "Web of Trust" where users can choose to either trust or distrust others. A user's personal Web of Trust includes his/her trusted users. Top reviewers and advisors are suggested to a user automatically if they are in his/her Web of Trust. The number of users who trust a given user will positively affect his/her status.

1.2.4   NEWS SITES

Users on news sites can post news and stories, and comment on them. Usually they also can rate news and comments posted by others, and these ratings are used by news sites to give more

---

[7]http://www.allexperts.com/
[8]http://www.askme.com/
[9]http://www.advogato.org/
[10]http://www.epinions.com/
[11]http://www.ciao.com/

visibility to posts and comments others appreciate and value. Two representative news sites are Kuro5hin[12] and Slashdot.[13]

Kuro5hin, started in 1999, provides an online platform to discuss technology and culture. Its users are allowed to post news and comments. The trust system on Kuro5hin is called Mojo and major changes had made to Kuro5bin in 2003 to improve its capability in handling posts from malicious users and avoid attacks to reduce the trustworthy score of targeted users. Those changes included that (1) it only allows a comment's score to influence a user's trustworthiness when there are at least six ratings contributing to it; and (2) it only allows one rating count from any single IP address. Slashdot is very similar to Kuro5hin. However, users in Slashdot can only rate comments and only editors can determine which stories appear on the homepage, which can avoid some attacks experienced by Kuro5hin. In addition, users in Slashdot are allowed to express an explicit trust statement by indicating others as friends if trust statements are positive or foes if trust statements are negative.

1.3   COMPUTATIONAL TASKS FOR TRUST

Trust has been extensively studied by many disciplines. However, social media data is very different from data other disciplines use to study trust. Hence, we need to further study trust in social media. First, the way social media data observed is very different. Social media users are distributed all over the world and it is difficult, if not impossible, to interact with them to gather information as other disciplines do. In other words, passive observation is the modus operandi for studying trust in social media. Second, social media data lacks necessary information other disciplines use to study trust. For example, in social media, most of sociometrics that a sociologist collects to study trust may not be available. Therefore, it is difficult to directly apply methods from other disciplines to study trust with social media data. Third, it is easy to collect social media data of hundreds of millions of users. In addition, social media data is big, noisy, sparse and incomplete, and novel computational tools are necessary in studying trust in social media. This book takes a computational perspective to offer an overview of characteristics and elements of trust and illuminate a wide range of computational tasks of trust in social media including representing trust, measuring trust, applying trust, and incorporating distrust, as shown in Figure 1.2. Next, we briefly introduce those tasks in trust computing.

1.3.1   REPRESENTING TRUST

As mentioned before, trust is a very complex concept. Hence, how to represent trust is an important and fundamental task in trust computing. Furthermore, algorithms of other computational tasks strongly depend on trust representations. For example, predicting trust under different types of context needs a multi-dimensional trust representation and multi-dimensional trust representations encourage social media applications based on trust circles. Representing trust aims to

---

[12]http://www.kuro5hin.org/
[13]http://slashdot.org/

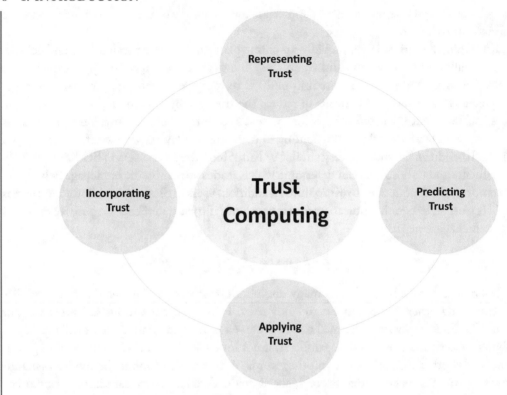

Figure 1.2: Four basic computational tasks of trust.

denote trust relations among users. An illustrative example is shown in Figure 1.3 where single-dimensional trust relations among users are denoted as a weighted trust network, which can be mathematically described as an adjacency matrix. More details about representing trust are discussed in Chapter 2.

Figure 1.3: Representing trust as a trust network and its corresponding adjacency matrix.

1.3.2   PREDICTING TRUST

The real-world trust networks are usually incomplete, indicating that many pairs of users in trust networks do not have explicit trust relations. That is especially true in social media since social media users are distributed world wide and the majority of them are not even connected. Trust relations in social media follow a power-law-like distribution—few users have a lot of trust relations while many users have a few trust relations. For example, the density of a typical trust network in social media is less than 0.01 [161]. The sparsity of trust relations in social media binders the applications of trust in social media, therefore predicting trust is necessarily inferring trust for those pairs without explicit trust relations by leveraging observed trust networks. Note that in this book predicting trust, inferring trust, measuring trust, and trust metrics are exchangeable. A typical example of predicting trust is demonstrated in Figure 1.4 where all known trust relations are given and it is asked to predict trust for those unknown pairs such as the trust value from user 1 to user 4 is predicted to 0.6. Various algorithms of predicting trust are discussed in Chapter 3.

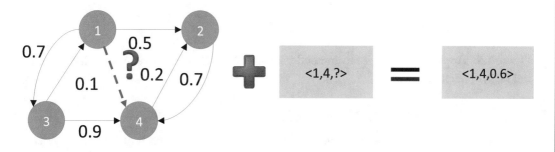

Figure 1.4: Predicting trust.

1.3.3   APPLYING TRUST

The information overload and credibility problems become increasingly severe in social media applications, and it is difficult for social media users to find relevant and reliable information. Trust can be applied to mitigate those problems because it provides necessary information about with whom we should share information and from whom we should collect information. Applying trust is to augment social media applications with trust, and recent years, trust is successfully adopted to help various social media applications such as recommendation, spam detection, and reputation systems. Recommender systems are one of the most successful applications of trust in social media, which cultivates a new research direction of recommendation, i.e., trust-aware recommender systems. A typical trust-aware recommender system is illustrated in Figure 1.5. Traditional recommender systems mainly utilize the rating information from users to items; while trust-aware recommender systems also exploit trust information among users in addition to rating information. We detail trust-aware recommender systems in Chapter 4.

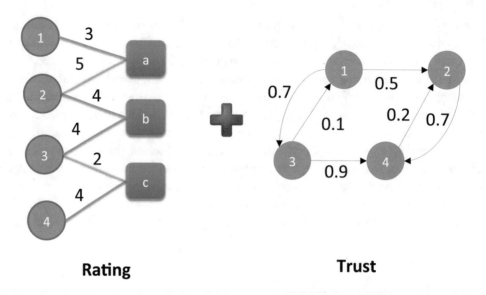

Rating   **Trust**

Figure 1.5: Applying trust in a recommender system. Note that in the figure, {1, 2, 3, 4} are users and {a, b, c} are items.

1.3.4   INCORPORATING DISTRUST

Without distrust, trust computing might be biased [127]. For example, for the adjacency matrix in Figure 1.3, a zero may denote there is no opinion from a user to another user, or there is a distrust relation between them although the former is a more common assumption. It is evident from various disciplines that distrust could be as important as trust especially for decision making and risk management. Therefore, distrust should be studied in trust computing. Incorporating distrust is to investigate how to incorporate distrust into tasks in trust computing including representing trust, predicting trust and applying trust, as shown in Figure 1.6. We introduce more details about incorporating distrust in Chapter 5.

1.4   SUMMARY

In this chapter we introduce definitions of trust in multiple disciplines, illustrate various types of online systems implementing trust mechanisms, discuss challenges for computing trust and define four computational tasks of trust in social media. This book provides an overall of trust from the computational perspective. But it should be pointed out that (1) though we cannot directly apply research achievements from other disciplines for social media data; however, those achievements such as social theories can help us derive computational models in various tasks of trust computing; and (2) there are many other trust-related topics we can not cover in this book such as relations among trust, security and privacy [113], and trust in cloud computing [66].

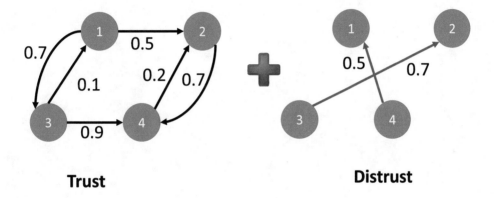

Figure 1.6: Incorporating distrust in trust computing.

CHAPTER 2

Representing Trust

Computational tasks of trust such as predicting trust, applying trust, and incorporating distrust are based on certain trust representations. Representing trust is the first and most important task to make trust computable. The properties of trust have been extensively and systematically studied, which serve as the foundation of trust representations. Each trust representation aims to capture certain properties of trust. For example, considering trust as a single concept is different from as a multi-dimensional concern. A multi-dimensional representation captures multi-dimensional properties of trust. In this chapter, we first introduce some key properties of trust with illustrations from real-world applications, and then present detailed representations of trust.

2.1 PROPERTIES OF TRUST

The properties of trust play an important role in various computational tasks of trust. In order to better understand these properties, we illustrate those properties with a social media dataset Epinions. This dataset contains 30,455 users, 363,773 trust relations and 46,196 distrust relations.

2.1.1 TRANSITIVITY

Transitivity is one of the most important properties of trust and allows trust to be propagated to reach other users. Transitivity of trust states that if user "Alice" trusts "Bob" and "Bob" trusts "Chuck" it can be inferred that "Alice" might also trust "Chuck" to some extent, as shown in Figure 2.1.

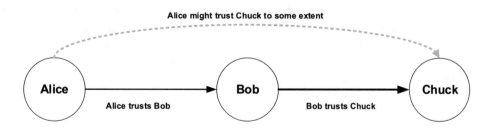

Figure 2.1: Transitivity of trust.

We examine the transitivity of trust in Epinions [138]. In that dataset, there are three possible relations from a user u_i to a user u_j including u_i trusting u_j (denoting as $u_i + u_j$), u_i

Table 2.1: Transitivity of trust. Note that $\langle u_i+u_j,u_j+u_k\rangle$ denotes two pairs of users where u_i trusts u_j and u_j trusts u_k

Types	Number	P1	P2
$\langle u_i+u_j,u_j+u_k\rangle,\ u_i?u_k$	25,584,525	88.34%	N.A
$\langle u_i+u_j,u_j+u_k\rangle,\ u_i+u_k$	3,320,991	11.46%	97.75%
$\langle u_i+u_j,u_j+u_k\rangle,\ u_i-u_k$	76,613	0.2%	2.25%

distrusting u_j (denoting as $u_i - u_j$), and a missing relation (denoting as $u_i?u_j$). For two pairs of users, $u_i + u_j$ and $u_j + u_k$, and we check possible relations between u_i and u_k. For the first calculation, we consider all (u_i, u_k) pairs (i.e., u_i+u_k, u_i-u_k, and $u_i?u_k$) and use "P1" to denote the percentage of pairs of (u_i, u_k) with a trust, a distrust or a missing relation over all pairs. For the second calculation, we only consider (u_i, u_k) pairs with observed relations (i.e., trust u_i+u_k and distrust u_i-u_k), and employ "P2" to represent the percentage of (u_i, u_k) with a trust or a distrust relation over pairs with observed relations (i.e., u_i+u_k and u_i-u_k). The results are shown in Table 2.1 and we can observe that 88.34% of pairs without relations. Hence, trust is not perfectly transitive according to the statistics; that is, if u_i highly trusts u_j, and u_j highly trusts u_k, it may not follow that u_i will highly trust u_k. This is especially true in social media. Users in social media trust networks are distributed world wide and there are many pairs of users who even do not know each other in trust networks. Therefore, trust networks in social media are usually very large and sparse. However, if we can observe a relation between u_i and u_k, it is likely to be a trust relation with 97.75%.

2.1.2   ASYMMETRY

Trust is a subjective and personal relation between users; hence for two users involved in a trust relation, trust is not necessarily identical in both directions. Since individuals have different experiences, and backgrounds, two users may not trust each other equally. For example, parents and children apparently trust one another differently, since parents and children are in different experience levels. From the network perspective, there are two understandings of the asymmetry about trust, as shown in Figure 2.2. If trust is binary, i.e., {trust, no trust}, asymmetry means one-way trust. For example, we observe that u trusts v; while there is no trust from v to u. If trust is continuous, i.e., continuous trust values, asymmetry means trust value from u to v could be different from that from v to u. For example, the trust value from u to v is 0.8 while that from v to u is 0.5.

We check the asymmetry of trust in the trust dataset Epinions from social media where the trust network is binary. In this case, we should observe many one-way trust relations. For each pair $u + v$, we check the relations from v to u and only 37.61% of pairs have mutual trust or 62.39% of trust relations are one-way trust relations. The impact of the number of trustors on the percentage of mutual trust has also been investigated. The percentage changes in terms of the

(a) Asymmetry for Trust with Binary Value

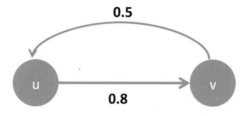

(b) Asymmetry for Trust with Continuous Value

Figure 2.2: Asymmetry of trust.

number of trustors are shown in Figure 2.3: a trustee with fewer number of trustors is more likely to trust their trustors back. In other words, trust becomes more and more asymmetric with the increase of the number of trustors [133].

2.1.3 COMPOSABILITY

Transitivity describes how trust can be propagated from one user to another user. In a social media trust network, there could be multiple paths connecting two users. Composability is another important property to measure trust by composing evidence from multiple sources, which can increase the confidence of trust measurements. Composability describes that a user should combine trust values received from different paths. As shown in Figure 2.4, there are two paths that Alice can use to infer trust information about Chuck, i.e., Alice-Bob-Chuck and Alice-Denise-Ed-Chuck. Composability of trust suggests that Alice should compose trust values from Alice-Bob-Chuck and Alice-Denise-Ed-Chuck for a more confident trust measurement about Chuck.

2.1.4 CORRELATION WITH SIMILARITY

We begin the discussion of this property with social correlation theories including homophily, social influence, and confounding, as shown in Figure 2.5.

- Homophily is to explain our tendency to connect to others that share certain similarity with us. For example, birds of a feather flock together [102].

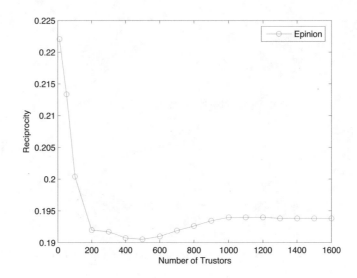

Figure 2.3: Asymmetry of trust with respect to the number of trustors.

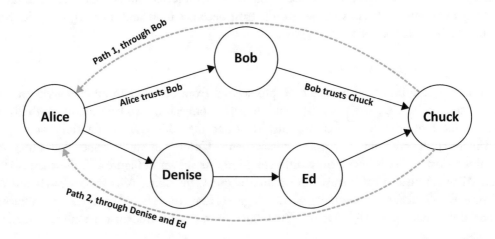

Figure 2.4: Composability of trust.

- Social influence suggests that people tend to follow the behaviors of their connected users and adjacent users are likely to exhibit similar behaviors [93]. For example, if most of one's friends switch to a mobile phone company, he could be influenced by them and switch, too.

- Confounding is a correlation between users that can also be forged due to external influences from environment. For example, two individuals living in the same city are more likely to become friends than two random individuals.

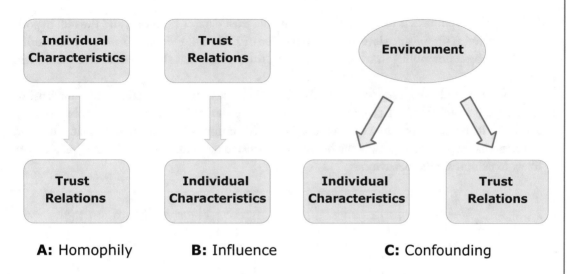

A: Homophily   **B:** Influence   **C:** Confounding

Figure 2.5: Social correlation theories.

There is a strong correlation between trust and similarity. The more similar two users are, the greater the trust exists between them [168]. Since trust is a type of social relations, this correlation can be explained by aforementioned social correlation theories. Next, we use homophily and social influence as examples to illustrate the existences of social correlations in trust.

Homophily: To verify the existence of homophily in trust, the following steps are usually performed:

- sorting trust relations based on their creating time stamps in chronological order;

- splitting data into m pieces with equal size and the divided time stamps are $\{t_1, t_2, \ldots, t_m\}$;

- dividing pairs of users without trust relations until t_i into two equal groups, i.e., high similarity group H and low similarity group L;

- computing the numbers of pairs creating trust relations h_i and l_i at time t_{i+1} for H and L, respectively;

- setting **h** as the vector of all $\{h_i\}$s and **l** as the vector of all $\{l_i\}$s; and

- conducting a two sample t-test on **h** and **l** where the null hypothesis is that pairs in low similarity groups create more trust relations; while the alternative hypothesis is that pairs in high similarity group create more trust relations as:

$$H_0 : \mathbf{l} \geq \mathbf{h}, \quad H_1 : \mathbf{l} < \mathbf{h}.$$

In [132], the hypothesis is tested on the social media trust dataset Epinions, and the null hypothesis is rejected at significance level 0.01 with p-value of 7.51e-64. Evidence from the t-test verifies the existence of homophily in trust: users tend to trust others that share certain similarities with them.

Influence: In [6], user cosine similarities are checked 100 days before and after trust relations were established in Epinions and the results are shown in Figure 2.6. It is observed that similarity increases before they trust each other, and continues to increase after that. The result suggests that users tend to follow the behaviors of trusted users and users with trust relations are likely to exhibit similar behaviors.

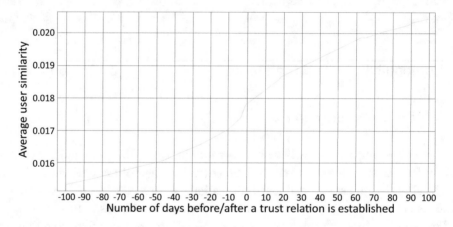

Figure 2.6: Influence in trust. This figure is from [6].

2.1.5 CONTEXT DEPENDENCE

Trust is context dependent. This means that trusting someone under one type of context does not guarantee trusting him in other types. For example, a user who is trustworthy in technology might not be also trustworthy in astronomy. The context dependence property of trust is studied in the real-world trust dataset Epinions. In Epinions, trust is used to indicate the reliability of users in item recommendations. Hence, context is chosen as the categories of items and some key findings about this property are presented as follows [133].

- In the studied six categories, less than 1% of users trust their friends in all categories. However, more than 70% of users trust their friends more than one category. On average, people trust only 35.4% of their trust networks for a specific category.

- Transitive and co-citation trust relationships are examined in Epinions. 22.3% of transitive trust relations are context dependent, while 13.1% of co-citation relations are context dependent. Examples of context dependent transitive and co-citation trust relationships are shown in Figure 2.7 where f_1 and f_2 are two types of context and we use different colors on the links to distinguish them. For example, a transitive trust relation, $i \rightarrow j \rightarrow k$, is context dependent where u_i trusts u_j in f_1, however, u_j trusts u_k in f_2; a co-citation trust, $i_1 \rightarrow j_2$ and $i_2 \rightarrow j_2$, is heterogeneous.

- Mutual trust relations are studied in the original network and 23.5% of these mutual relations are context dependent. For example, the trust relations $i \rightarrow k$ and $k \rightarrow i$ are different types as shown in Figure 2.8.

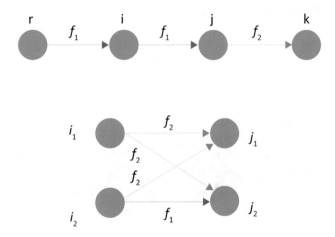

Figure 2.7: Heterogeneous transitive and co-citation trust relations. Note that f_1 and f_2 are two types of context and we use different colors on the links to distinguish them.

2.1.6   DYNAMIC

Trust is sensitive to be influenced and it is usually changed with time [153]. There are many factors which can lead to the evolution of trust such as events, changes of context or the changing conditions of the environment such as adding new users and introducing new features to online trust systems. In [134], the properties of context dependence and dynamic are investigated simultaneously in Epinions and the trust evolution speed under different types of context is demonstrated in Figure 2.9. Key observations about the dynamics of trust include: (1) users change their trust very different; and (2) trust is very dynamic under some types of context, while it is relatively stable under others.

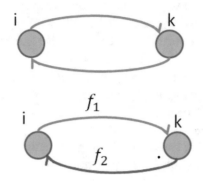

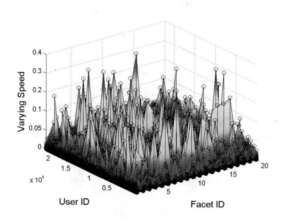

Figure 2.8: Heterogeneous mutual trust relations. Note that f_1 and f_2 are two types of context.

Figure 2.9: Trust evolution speed under different types of context.

2.2   TRUST REPRESENTATIONS

Trust representations can be classified from different perspectives including an interpretation perspective and a dimension perspective:

- from an interpretation perspective, trust is naturally interpreted as either probabilistic or gradual representations; and

- from a dimension perspective, trust representations can be classified into single-dimensional and multi-dimensional representations.

2.2.1   PROBABILISTIC VS. GRADUAL REPRESENTATIONS

Probabilistic Representations

Probabilistic models deal with a single trust value in a binary way (or a user can either be trusted or not). It computes a probability that a user can be trusted. A higher trust value suggested by probabilistic representations corresponds to a higher probability that a user can be trusted. In probabilistic representations, a triple $< u_1, u_2, p >$ denotes the probability p of u_1 trusting u_2. Since p denotes a probability, the value of p is between 0 and 1 where $p = 1$ represents full trust while $p = 0$ indicates no trust. The probability p usually is assumed to follow certain distributions such as beta distribution [63]. For example, if we assume that trust values follow a beta distribution, the probability of user i trusting user j is calculated as:

$$\mathbf{T}_{ij} = \frac{pos + 1}{pos + neg + 2},$$

where pos and neg are the number of positive and negative ratings from u_i to u_j. The probabilistic representations provide a natural representation for users to express their uncertainty and allow users to exchange, combine and filter trust received from other users. If we represent these triples from probabilistic representations into a trust network, the trust network is a complete and weighted graph as shown in Figure 2.10 where weights in the trust network represent the probabilities of the existence of links in the network. Note that in practice, we usually remove these links with probability 0 from the network in Figure 2.10. Similar to denoting a network into an adjacency matrix, a probabilistic representation can be denoted by an adjacency matrix, as shown in Figure 2.10. The values of the matrix is in [0, 1] and the entity in the i-th row and the j-th column represents the probability of u_i trusting u_j.

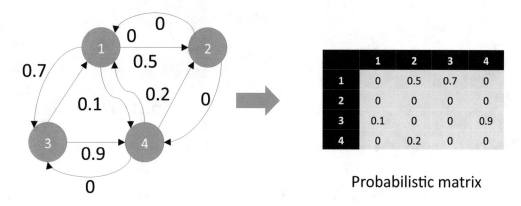

Figure 2.10: An illustrative example of probabilistic representations.

Gradual Representations

In reality, trust is often interpreted as a gradual phenomenon—humans trust others rarely in a binary way, i.e., trusting and not trusting someone, but often in a gradual way, i.e., trusting someone very much, more or less, and little. Gradual representations become popular in recent years. In gradual representations, trust values can be any values so they cannot be explained as probabilities. A high trust value indicates a higher trust in a user, which makes the ordering of trust values a very important factor. Fuzzy logic can be naturally used as a gradual trust representation since it represents vague intervals rather than exact values. For instance, in [76], fuzzy linguistic terms present trust in agents in a P2P network; and fuzzy cognitive maps, a combination of fuzzy logic and neural networks, are developed in [72] to represent trust. A representative system implementing a gradual trust representation can be found in [1] where a four-value scale is used to determine the trustworthiness of agents, i.e., very trustworthy, trustworthy, untrustworthy and very untrustworthy. A triple $< u_1, u_2, t >$ denotes that the trust value between u_1 and u_2 is t. The value of p in probabilistic representations is limited in [0, 1], while the value of t in gradual representations can be any values. If we represent those triples in gradual representations into a trust network, the trust network is an incomplete and weighted graph, as shown in Figure 2.11 where weights in the trust network denote trust values and there is on link for pairs if the trust value is zero. Similarly, the trust network can be denoted as an adjacency matrix. Its value could be any real numbers such as 1.7 in Figure 2.11 and the entity of its i-th row and j-th column represents the trust value from user i to user j.

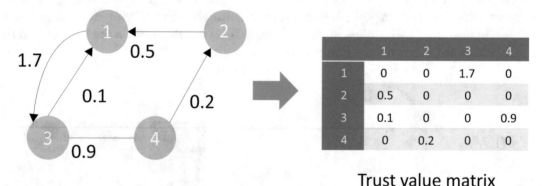

Trust value matrix

Figure 2.11: An illustrative example of gradual representations.

2.2.2 SINGLE-DIMENSIONAL VS. MULTI-DIMENSIONAL REPRESENTATIONS

Aforementioned trust representations assume single trust relations between users. However, trust is one of the most complex social concepts and usually has multiple dimensions. For example, trust is context dependent hence trusting someone on one type of context does not necessarily mean that he should be trusted on others [133], while trust could be very different when using different evaluation metrics such as cost and quality [43]. In this subsection, we introduce two multi-dimensional trust presentations including context-dependent multi-dimensional trust and evaluation-dependent multi-dimensional trust.

We can denote single-dimensional trust in an adjacency matrix. However, the matrix is not sufficient to represent multi-dimensional trust; hence a *tensor*, also known as multidimensional matrix, is introduced for multi-dimensional trust. An Nth-order tensor $\mathcal{A}$ is denoted as $\mathcal{A} \in \mathbb{R}^{I_1 \times I_2 \times \ldots \times I_N}$ where I_j is the size of the j-th dimensions and usually 3rd-order tensor is powerful enough for the vast majority of multi-dimensional trust, as shown in Figure 2.12. Context-dependent multi-dimensional trust expends the matrix with an extra dimension to denote different types of context; while evaluation-based multi-dimensional trust expends the matrix with an extra dimension to denote different evaluation metrics.

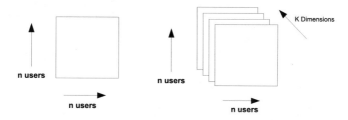

Figure 2.12: Matrix for single-dimensional trust vs. tensor for multi-dimensional trust. Note that dimensions in context-dependent multi-dimensional trust denote types of context; while dimensions in evaluation-based multi-dimensional trust denote metrics.

Context-dependent Multi-dimensional Representations of Trust

People's multifaceted interests and experts of different types suggest that people may place trust differently to others under different types of context, i.e., trust is context dependent. Take a specific topic, like item recommendation, as an example. Users may be able to form a general opinion about how much they trust others about recommendations, but it would be more accurate and specific to break that trust down by categories. We may trust a friend about items in "Restaurants," but not about "Home & Garden." Figure 2.13 demonstrates an example in Epinions. Figure 2.13(a) demonstrates single-dimensional trust relations between a real user from Epinions,[1] represented by user 1, and her 20 representative friends. Figures 2.13(b), 2.13(c), and 2.13(d) show their trust relations in the categories of "Home & Garden," "Restaurants," and "Kids and Family," respectively. The width of arcs in these figures indicates their trust strengths. The top 3 trustworthy people in Figures 2.13(a), 2.13(b), 2.13(c), and 2.13(d) are users {7, 8, 18}, {19, 8, 6}, {7, 9, 11}, and {7, 8, 17}, respectively. They are very different from one another; thus trust under different categories can be different.

[1]http://www.epinions.com/user-nancy35c

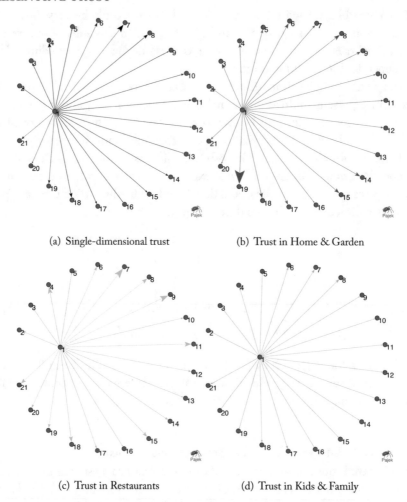

(a) Single-dimensional trust

(b) Trust in Home & Garden

(c) Trust in Restaurants

(d) Trust in Kids & Family

Figure 2.13: Context-dependent multi-dimensional trust.

A trust relation in a context-dependent trust representation is denoted as a quadruple $<u, v, c, p>$. The quadruple $<u, v, c, p>$ denotes that the trust from u to v under the context c is p where p is the probability if we choose probabilistic models or trust value if we choose gradual models . Next we introduce two representative context dependent trust representations.

mTrust is a multi-dimensional representation to capture trust relations of users in the context of categories for recommender systems [133]. The intuition behind mTrust is that a user, who trusts recommendations from another user in one category, may not trust him/her in other categories. mTrust extends the user-user trust matrix to a 3rd-order tensor by adding categories as an extra dimension.

In e-commerce such as eBay and Taobao, reputation scores are usually high for sellers, known as the "all good reputation" problem [166], and it becomes difficult for buyers to choose sellers. Buyers often express their opinions via comments, which contain mixed opinions regarding different aspects of transactions. For example, a user positively rated a transaction, while left the following comment "bad communication, will not buy from again. super slow ship(ping). item as described." Apparently the user has negative opinions with respect to communication and delivery, although an overall positive rating toward the transaction. Those observations suggest that multi-dimensional trust can more accurately describe the real situations in e-commerce. Hence, a multi-dimension trust Commtrust [166] is proposed to capture context-dependent trust by mining comments in transactions in e-commerce. It extends the user-user single-dimensional trust matrix to a 3rd-order tensor by adding aspects of transactions as an extra dimension.

Evaluation-dependent Multi-dimensional Representations of Trust
Trust is subjective and trust could be very different since users evaluate the trustworthiness of others along multiple metrics. Evaluation-dependent multi-dimensional trust representations often extend a matrix representation to a 3rd-order tensor representation by adding metrics as an extra dimension. Different evaluation-dependent multi-dimensional trust representations choose different types of metrics to assess trust. Next, we introduce several representative metrics for evaluation-dependent multi-dimensional representations of trust.

Castelfranchi and Falcone consider trust as encompassing beliefs about competence, disposition, dependence, and fulfillment [16]. There are four entities in the B2C e-commerce such as Amazon including consumer, seller, third party, and technology, and based on the B-to-C market structure and the interactions of those four entities, several metrics are defined to assess trust in [67] as:

- Consumer-behavioral dimension: individual attributes that affect the trusting behaviors of consumers.

- Institutional dimension: third parties and other institutional attributes that shape the institutional environment.

- Information content dimension: attributes of a product that promote or deter online exchange.

- Transaction dimension: attributes that make online transactions trustworthy.

- Technology dimension: information system and software attributes that enable the online exchange to be effective and safe.

Four metrics are defined in [43] to evaluate the trust of a user.

- Success: it evaluates the likelihood that a user will successfully execute a task.

- Cost: it assesses the likelihood that the cost of executing the task will be no more than expected.

- Timeliness: it evaluates the likelihood that a user will complete the task no later than expected.

- Quality: it assesses the likelihood that the quality of results provided by a user will meet expectations.

2.3   RECENT ADVANCES OF TRUST REPRESENTATIONS

Since trust is one of the most important social concepts; many advanced trust representations are developed to capture various trust relations among users. Next we introduce some advanced trust representations.

2.3.1   DIMENSION CORRELATION

The vast majority of multi-dimensional trust representations assume the independence of dimensions. However, these dimensions typically exhibit correlations. Different types of context in context-dependent trust may be correlated such as the category "electronics" and the category "computers" in the mTrust study [133]. Similarly, correlations may also arise in metrics for evaluation-based trust. In [115], trust representations are developed to capture correlations among dimensions.

2.3.2   TEMPORAL INFORMATION

Most of aforementioned trust representations assume static trust relationships between users. However, trust is inherently dynamic and it evolves as humans interact based on the findings from social sciences. Recently, eTrust is developed to capture trust evolution in social media [134]. eTrust extends mTrust from a 3rd-order tenor to a fourth-order tensor by adding temporal information as a new dimension. A trust relation is represented as $< u, v, c, p, t >$ by eTrust; and it suggests the trust from u to v under the context of c is denoted as p at time t where p is either a probability or a trust value.

2.3.3   TRUST, UNTRUST, AND DISTRUST

Untrust (or no trust) and distrust are not the same [127]. The former means that there is no evaluation from one user to another; the latter distrust shows that there is a distrust evaluation from one user to another. However, the vast majority of trust representations cannot distinguish untrust and distrust, since the trust values of untrust and distrust are often represented as zeros in trust representations. An advanced trust representation should incorporate distrust and more details about trust representations with distrust are discussed in Chapter 5.

CHAPTER 3

Predicting Trust

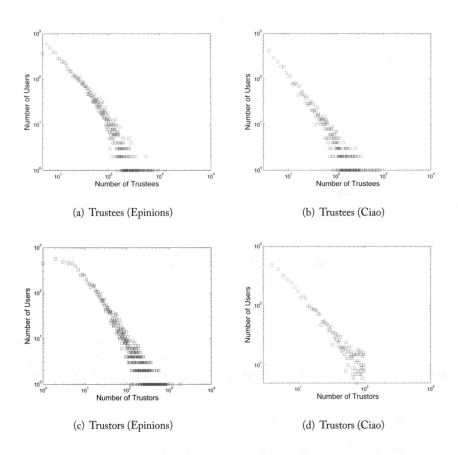

(a) Trustees (Epinions)　　　　　　　　(b) Trustees (Ciao)

(c) Trustors (Epinions)　　　　　　　　(d) Trustors (Ciao)

Figure 3.1: Trustor and trustee distributions of trust networks from Epinions and Ciao.

For trust networks in social media, users are distributed world wide and they only have trust relations with a small number of users; in other words, most of user pairs do not have explicit trust relations. The distributions of trustees and trustors for users in two social media trust networks, i.e., Epinions and Ciao, are depicted in Figure 3.1. Those distributions suggest that the explicit trust relations are extremely sparse and follow a power-law distribution: a small number of users specify many trust relations while a large proportion of users specify a few trust relations. For a very small trust network, it is possible to ask its users to assess trustworthiness of others, which becomes difficult or even impossible for large-scale trust networks in social media. Therefore, the task of predicting trust (or trust metric) is proposed to predict or infer how much a certain user can be trusted by the other users automatically when there are no explicit trust relations between them, and it is an important task to mitigate the problem of sparseness in user-specified trust relations for trust computing.

3.1   BASIC CONCEPTS

3.1.1   DEFINITION

A trust metric measures how much a certain user can be trusted by the other users for the community and it is also referred to a machine learning technique of measuring, inferring, or predicting trust. We use $\mathbf{T} \in \mathbb{R}^{n \times n}$ to denote trust relations of n users where $\mathbf{T}_{ij}$ denotes trust from u_i to u_j. Let $\mathcal{T} = \{(u_i, u_j) | \mathbf{T}_{ij} \neq 0\}$ be the set of pairs of users with explicit trust relations and $\mathcal{U} = \{(u_i, u_j | \mathbf{T}_{ij} = 0)\}$ be the set of pairs of users without explicit trust relations. For trust networks in social media, the number of pairs in $\mathcal{U}$ is usually much larger than that in $\mathcal{T}$, and the ratio of $\frac{|\mathcal{U}|}{|\mathcal{U}| + |\mathcal{T}|}$ is often larger than 0.99. Formally, a trust metric is to predict or infer trust values for pairs in $\mathcal{U}$ by leveraging trust values of pairs of users in $\mathcal{T}$. The basic assumptions about trust metrics are the propagation and composability of trust: (1) you are more likely to trust your trustees than a stranger and a trustee of your trustee is possibly more trustworthy than a random stranger; and (2) you can research others via multiple paths and trust aggregated from multiple paths is more accurate.

3.1.2   CLASSIFICATIONS OF TRUST METRICS

Trust metrics were originally designed to support Public Key Infrastructure and later on developed to various research fields such as P2P networks, mobile computing, ratings systems, and social media. Therefore, trust metrics can be classified and characterized from different perspectives as follows [139].

- From a personalization perspective, trust metrics can be classified as global and local metrics.

- From a methodology perspective, trust metrics can be characterized as unsupervised and supervised metrics.

- From a distribution perspective, trust metrics can be binary and continuous metrics.

Global and Local Trust Metrics
Trust metrics can be categorized into global an local metrics from a personalization perspective. Global trust metrics predict the same trust of a given user for all users, i.e., predicting a global trust value for each user. In some applications, we also refer to global trust values as reputation scores

or status scores. To calculate global trust scores, global trust metrics usually need to access the whole trust networks. Formally, a global trust metric aims to compute a global trust score p_i for each user u_i in a given trust network. In reality, it may be difficult to reach an agreement among the users regarding another user. Users may have completely different opinions about the same users, i.e., users' trust opinions may be personalized. Hence, local metrics provide a personalized trust score that depends on the point of view of the evaluating user and they compute a trust value $\mathbf{T}_{ij}$ for each pair of users (u_i, u_j) without explicit trust relations. If we represent trust relations among users as a trust network, the differences of global and local trust metrics are demonstrated in Figure 3.2.

- Global trust metrics focus on the nodes (or the users) of the network and compute a trust value for each node, as shown in Figure 3.2(a). In the figure, we use the size of a node to denote its trust value and the larger the size, the higher the trust value. A global trust metric computes a trust value for each node, while leading to the changes of the size of nodes.

- Local metrics focus on pairs of nodes (or users) without explicit trust relations in the network, as shown in Figure 3.2(b). A local trust metric suggests some pairs of users with trust relations such as a trust relation from u_4 to u_2 and a trust relation from u_3 to u_1.

In a trust network with n users, global metrics need to compute a trust value for each user hence n global trust values in total, thus it is efficient to compute and maintain. It is suitable to apply global trust metrics in those systems needing a global view about a user's reputation such as reputation systems and voting systems. While local trust metrics calculate trust values for pairs of users without explicit trust relations and there are potentially n^2 pairs of users in a trust network with n users. Users may have very different trust opinions on the same users especially on those controversial users and local trust metrics are very useful in those scenarios. Local trust metrics are widely applied to those systems which need personalized trust values such as recommender systems and information filtering systems. In this book, we consider reputation and global trust equivalently. However, reputation and trust are different concepts since reputation is global while trust can be global or local. Reputation is not necessarily equal to local trust, which can be illustrated by the following statements: (1) I trust you due to your good reputation; and (2) I trust you despite your bad reputation. More discussions about reputation and trust can be found in [62].

Supervised and Unsupervised Trust Metrics

From a methodology perspective, trust metrics can be classified as supervised and unsupervised metrics. Supervised metrics consider trust prediction as a classification problem. As we know, one disadvantage for a typical classification problem is that we need sufficient training samples to obtain a good classifier, which is very time- and effort-consuming in practice. However, since the existence of trust can be naturally treated as label information, no extra labeling efforts are needed. Unsupervised metrics predict trust based on certain properties of trust such as transitivity

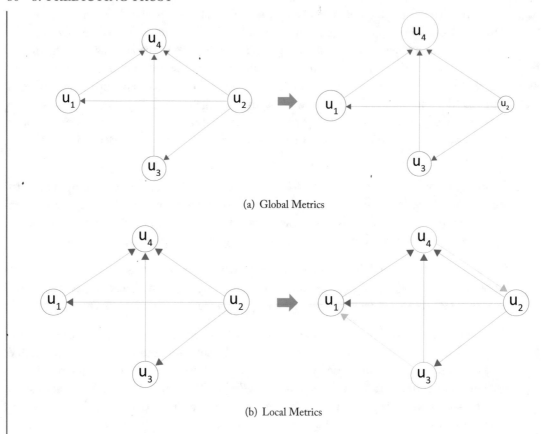

(a) Global Metrics

(b) Local Metrics

Figure 3.2: Global and local trust metrics. Note that the size of nodes denotes their trustworthy scores and trust relations with green colors represent new relations. Global metrics compute trust scores for nodes, which affect the size of nodes, while local trust metrics calculate trust values for pairs of nodes without explicit trust relations, which predict new trust relations.

and low-rank representations. If we consider trust relations as a trust network, supervised trust metrics use links of the network as labels, while unsupervised trust metrics use the topological structures and properties of the network.

In supervised scenarios, we always consider pairs with trust as positive samples while pairs without trust as negative samples. In a typical trust network in social media, the number of negative samples is much larger than that of positive samples, or supervised trust metrics are highly imbalanced classification problems. A key to the success of supervised trust metrics is to extract proper features to represent pairs of users; hence, supervised trust metrics always make use of extra sources to construct features to represent pairs of users. Supervised trust metrics have their advantages: they usually outperform unsupervised metrics, are easily adopted to different domains, and can perform predictions for users with few or even no trust relations. Unsupervised metrics are based on topological structures and properties of the trust network and strongly depend on the existing trust relations; hence it may fail for users with few trust relations. However, unsupervised metrics have no imbalanced-sample problems and can be naturally applied to trust with both binary and continuous values.

Binary and Continuous Trust Metrics

From a distribution perspective, trust metrics can be classified as binary and continuous trust metrics. Binary metrics are used to predict whether users are trusted or not trusted, i.e., the existence of trust for pairs of users where 1 denotes that there is trust and 0 denotes that there is no trust; while continuous trust metrics are to infer continuous trust values for pairs of users. Formally, binary trust metrics assign trust values in $\{0, 1\}$ while continuous trust metrics assign any real numbers as trust values. If we represent trust relations as a trust network, binary trust metrics work with a binary trust network whose adjacency matrix is a binary matrix while continuous trust metrics work with a weighted trust network whose adjacency matrix is a continuous matrix, as shown in Figure 3.3.

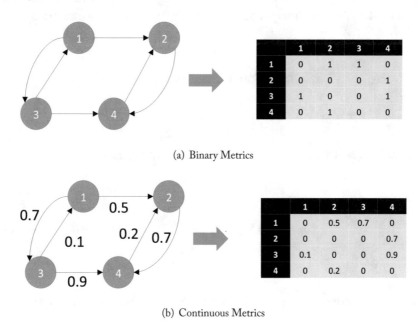

(a) Binary Metrics

(b) Continuous Metrics

Figure 3.3: Binary and continuous trust metrics. Binary trust metrics work with a binary trust network; while continuous trust metrics work with a weighted trust network.

3.1.3 A UNIFIED CLASSIFICATION OF TRUST METRICS

The aforementioned three classifications of trust metrics can have network understandings, and we may develop a unified classification of trust metrics from the network perspective. A trust network contains a set of nodes and a set of trust relations. Among the aforementioned six types of trust metrics, only global trust metrics compute trust values for nodes, while others focus on pairs of users without explicit trust relations in the trust network. Local trust metrics can be supervised or unsupervised and both supervised and unsupervised trust metrics could be binary and continuous. Therefore, a unified classification of trust metrics is shown in Figure 3.4: we first divide trust metrics into global and local metrics according to their focuses; then we further divide local metrics into supervised and unsupervised metrics according to their methodologies and finally either supervised or unsupervised metrics can be binary and continuous. Most supervised trust metrics are binary. To apply supervised metrics to continuous trust, we need to discretize continuous trust values as a pre-processing step. While the vast majority of unsupervised trust metrics are continuous. To apply unsupervised metrics on binary trust, we first perform unsupervised metrics to obtain continuous trust values and then use a threshold to determine trust or no trust as a post-processing. Therefore, when we review algorithms of trust metrics in the following section, we do not further divide supervised and unsupervised metrics into binary and continuous metrics.

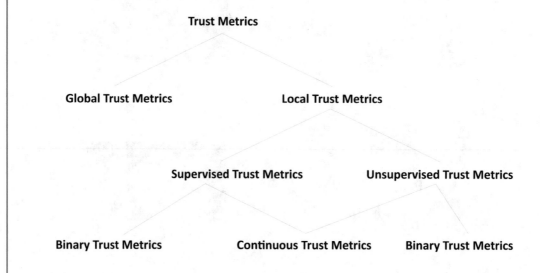

Figure 3.4: A unified classification of trust metrics.

3.2   ALGORITHMS OF TRUST METRICS

According to the unified classification of trust metrics, we first introduce global trust metrics and then local trust metrics with supervised and unsupervised settings.

3.2.1   GLOBAL TRUST METRICS

For each user in a given trust network, a global trust is to compute a trustworthy score (or a reputation score) based on the topological structure of the given trust network. Representative global trust metrics such as Eigentrust [64], Peertrust [152], and Powertrust [167] are inherited the basic idea from Pagerank. If u_i wants to know the trust she should put on u_k, she can ask trust opinions from his trustees u_j. Let $\mathbf{t}_i$ be the trust score vector for u_i and $\mathbf{c}_i$ be the initial trust score vector. Eigentrust performs the following iterative aggregating process:

- u_i asks his/her direct trustees:

$$\mathbf{t}_i = \mathbf{T}^\top \mathbf{c}_i;$$

- u_i asks his/her trustees' trustees:

$$\mathbf{t} = (\mathbf{T}^\top)^2 \mathbf{c}_i; \quad \text{and}$$

- u_i keeps asking until convergence:

$$\mathbf{t} = (\mathbf{T}^\top)^N \mathbf{c}_i,$$

where $\mathbf{T}$ is the normalized adjacency matrix with $\sum_j \mathbf{T}_{ij} = 1$. When N is large, $\mathbf{t}_i$, $i \in \{1, 2, \ldots, n\}$ converges to the same vector $\mathbf{t}$ for every user where $\mathbf{t}$ is the first eigenvector of $\mathbf{T}$ as:

$$\mathbf{t}^{(k+1)} = \mathbf{T}^\top \mathbf{t}^k. \tag{3.1}$$

In fact, Eq. (3.1) is the basic version of Pagerank in the form of matrix. Pagerank [110] calculated the trustworthy score t_i of u_i by aggregating trustworthy scores from u_i's trustors:

$$t_i = \sum_j t_j \frac{\mathbf{T}_{ij}}{\sum_k \mathbf{T}_{jk}},$$

where a trustor's trustworthy score is shared by all her trustees. The convergence of the basic formulation of PageRank is guaranteed only if $\mathbf{T}$ is irreducible and aperiodic. The latter is guaranteed in practice for real-world networks, while the former is true if we add a damping factor $1 - \alpha$ to the rank propagation as:

$$t_i = \alpha \sum_j t_j \frac{\mathbf{T}_{ij}}{\sum_k \mathbf{T}_{jk}} + (1 - \alpha)\mathbf{p},$$

where a typical choice of $\mathbf{p}$ is $\mathbf{p} = [\frac{1}{n}]_{n \times 1}$. This modification improves the quality of PageRank by introducing a decay factor $1 - \alpha$ which limits the effect of rank sinks. The above formulations treat all trustees equally when distributing scores. However, the importance of both trustors and trustees might be different. The more popular users are, the more trust relations that other users tend to establish with them or are established by them. Weighted Pagerank [151] assigns larger trust values to more important (popular) users instead of dividing the trust value of a user evenly among its trustees. Each trustee gets a trust value proportional to its popularity (its number of trustors and trustees). The popularity of trustors and trustees is denoted as W_{ij}^o and W_{ij}^e below.

- W_{ij}^o is the weight of the trust relation from u_i to u_j calculated based on the number of trustors of u_i and the number of trustees of u_j as:

$$W_{ij}^o = \frac{I_i}{\sum_{u_p \in \Gamma_j} I_p},$$

  where I_i and I_p represent the number of trustors of u_i and u_p, respectively, and Γ_j denotes the set of trustors of u_i.

- W_{ij}^e is the weight of the trust relation from u_i to u_j calculated based on the number of trustees of u_i and the number of trustors of u_j as:

$$W_{ij}^e = \frac{O_i}{\sum_{u_p \in \Gamma_j} O_p},$$

  where O_i and O_p represent the number of trustees of u_i and u_p, respectively.

With the definitions of W_{ij}^o and W_{ij}^e, weighted Pagerank takes into account the importance of trustors and trustees, and distributes trustworthy scores based on the popularity of users, which is formulated as:

$$t_i = \alpha \sum_j t_j W_{ij}^o W_{ij}^e + (1 - \alpha)\mathbf{p},$$

Aforementioned various formulations for PageRank and its variants, a single PageRank vector is computed, independent of any particular context. The trustworthiness of users might be very different under different types of context. For example, a user is trustworthy for "sports" but she is not necessarily trustworthy for "computer." Therefore, to yield more accurate trust metrics, top-sensitive Pagerank algorithm is proposed, which computes a set of PageRank vectors, biased using a set of representative topics [49]. In addition to metrics based on Pagerank, there are also many global trust metrics based on Belief models [158] and Fuzzy models [117]. An overall of these models can be found in [62].

3.2.2   LOCAL TRUST METRICS

For a pair of users without explicit trust relations in a given trust network, local trust metrics aim to refer a trust value for the pair. Local trust metrics can be roughly divided into two groups: supervised methods as shown in Figure 3.5 and unsupervised methods as demonstrated in Figure 3.6. Supervised metrics first extract features from available sources and consider the existence of trust relations as labels, then train a binary classifier and finally predict the label of a given pair by the classifier, while unsupervised metrics depend on topological properties of trust such as propagation in Figure 3.6(a) and the low-rank structure in Figure 3.6(b).

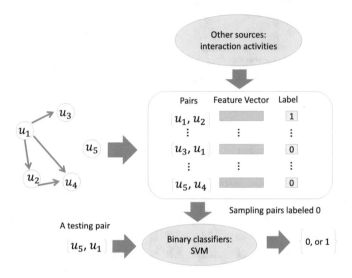

Figure 3.5: An illustration of supervised trust metrics.

Supervised Trust Metrics

Supervised trust metrics consider trust prediction as a classification problem. For a typical classification problem, there are two important preprocessing steps. One is to extract features to represent pairs of users without trust relations (or data representation) and the other is to prepare training data (or training data preparation). The latter is trivial since trust relations can be naturally considered as class labels. Different supervised methods basically vary with their data representations (or they extract different feature sets to represent data). The given trust network is often not sufficient for supervised methods to extract features; hence, the vast majority of supervised methods use extra sources such as user profiles, user-generated content, and user interactions.

Among many reasons that a user trusts another user, one is that the trustee has good reputation and another is that there have been good personal interactions between those two users. In [84], a taxonomy is developed to systematically organize an extensive set of features for pre-

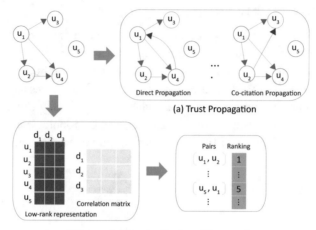

(a) Trust Propagation

(b) Low-rank Approximation based Framework

Figure 3.6: An illustration of unsupervised trust metrics

dicting trust relations. It extracts two sets of features, i.e., user factors and interaction factors, which correspond to the aforementioned two reasons, respectively. User factors contain rater-related, writer-related, or commenter-related, and interaction features capture various interactions between the users. It chooses SVM and NB classifier as its basic classifiers. By assessing the importance of those two sets of features, Liu et al. found that trust is highly relevant to user interactions since interaction factors have greater impact on trust decisions than user factors do.

In management science, a trust antecedent framework as shown in Figure 3.7 indicates that: (1) ability, benevolence, and integrity are key factors that lead to trust on a trustee; (2) trust propensity is a factor that determines how easy a trustor trusts someone; (3) once a trust is formed, the trustor is willing to take more risk; and (4) the outcome of risk taking will serve as feedback to modify the perception about trustee's ability, benevolence, and integrity. Viet-An Nguyen et al. [109] proposed various trust prediction models based on this well-studied Trust Antecedent Framework in management science. Similar to [84], each factor is approximated through a set of quantitative features. For example, the features for integrity are called trustworthiness, equal to the number of trust statements the user receives while ability related factors are the features that compute the average rating given by a rater to the reviews written by a particular reviewer and the number of reviews rated by the rater.

In [92], various features based on writer-reviewer interactions are extracted and used in personalized and cluster-based classification methods. Nikolay Korovaiko et al. [70] focused on a case where the background data are user ratings for online products and observe that state-of-the-art classifiers can achieve very good performance in predicting trust based on extracted features, which capture the following factors for a pair of users (u_i, u_j):

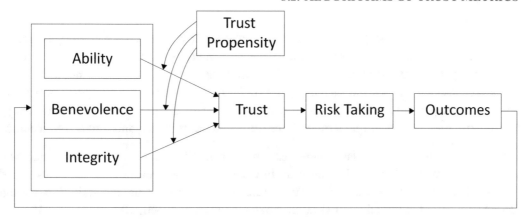

Figure 3.7: A trust antecedent framework in management science.

- u_i and u_j give similar ratings to the reviews they read;

- u_i and u_j are interested in similar categories of products;

- u_i and u_j produce reviews in the same categories that interest them;

- u_i and u_j rate the reviews produced by the same reviewers;

- u_i and u_j have the same trustees;

- u_i gives high ratings to reviews produced by u_j;

- u_i anonymizes a considerable number of ratings for reviews produced by v_j; and

- u_j is a reputable reviewer

Kiyana Zolfaghar et al. [171] provided a framework of social trust-inducing factors that contribute in trust formation process and then investigated the role of these factors in predicting trust between users.

Unsupervised Trust Metrics
Unsupervised methods are usually based on certain topological properties of the given trust/distrust networks. Algorithms in this family can be further divided into similarity-based, propagation-based, and low-rank approximation-based methods according to their adopted topological properties of trust.

Similarity-based Methods

Ziegler et al. [168] investigated the connection between user similarity (such as ratings of movies) and trust. They found a strong and significant correlation between trust and similarity. The more similar two people are, the greater the trust between them is. Similarity-based methods first calculate user-user similarities and then use those similarities to indicate the likelihood of trust relations. According to sources that we use to measure similarity, there are three representative types of similarity measures including structural measure, content measure, and interaction measure.

Structural Measure: It calculates user-user similarity based on the topological structure of the given trust networks. It is used to measure how close two users are in trust networks and the intuition behind this measure is that if two users are close in the trust network, they are more likely to establish trust relations. Below are three representative methods.

- *Normalized Common Trustors.* For a pair of users (u_i, u_j) without a explicit trust relation, the normalized common trustors is formally defined as

$$Sim(i, j) = \frac{|\Gamma_i \cap \Gamma_j|}{|\Gamma_i|},$$

  where Γ_i is the set of trustors of u_i. Note that a similar method can be developed for *normalized common trustees.*

- *Jaccard's coefficient on Trustors.* Jaccard's coefficient on trustors is defined as the number of shared trustors of two users divided by the total number of their unique trustors. Specifically, for a pair of users (u_i, u_j), Jaccard's coefficient on trustor is formally defined as

$$Sim(i, j) = \frac{|\Gamma_i \cap \Gamma_j|}{|\Gamma_i \cup \Gamma_j|}.$$

- *Katz Score.* For a pair of users (u_i, u_j), it sums all possible paths from u_i to u_j with exponential damping by length to weight short paths more heavily as,

$$Sim(i, j) = \sum_{\ell=1}^{\infty} \beta^\ell |path_{i,j}^\ell|,$$

  where $path_{i,j}^\ell$ is the set of paths from u_i to u_j with length ℓ and damping factor β is typically set to 0.05.

  The Katz scores for all pairs of users $\mathbf{K} \in \mathbb{R}^{n \times n}$ in a trust network with n users can be computed in the matrix form through its adjacency matrix $\mathbf{T}$ as

$$\mathbf{K} = \sum_{\ell=1}^{\infty} \beta^\ell \mathbf{T}^\ell = (\mathbf{I}_n - \beta \mathbf{T})^{-1} - \mathbf{I}_n,$$

where $\mathbf{I}_n$ is the $n \times n$ identity matrix.

Content Measure: Homophily is one of the most important theories that attempt to explain why people establish trust relations with each other. The homophily effect suggests that similar users have a higher likelihood to establish trust relations. Hence the similarity of user generated content could be an important indicator of trust relations. Assume that we can extract a set of M features $\mathcal{F} = \{f_1, f_2, \ldots, f_M\}$ to represent each user as $\mathbf{u}_i \in \mathbb{R}^M$ where $\mathbf{u}_{ij}$ is the feature value of f_j for u_i. For a pair of users (u_i, u_j), their content similarity could be defined as the cosine similarity of $\mathbf{u}_i$ and $\mathbf{u}_j$ as:

$$Sim(u_i, u_j) = \frac{\sum_k \mathbf{u}_{ik} \cdot \mathbf{u}_{jk}}{\sqrt{\sum_k \mathbf{u}_{ik}^2} \sqrt{\sum_k \mathbf{u}_{jk}^2}}.$$

Interaction Measure: In a typical trust network, there are tens of hundreds of nodes (or users). A user is likely to communicate or interact more frequently with her trusted users than strangers. For example, in the context of product review sites, users tend to rate the helpfulness of reviews from their trusted users more frequently, and in eBay, buyers have more purchase transactions from their trusted users. Therefore, interaction activities provide strong possible indicators for trust.

Let $\mathcal{I} = \{I_1, I_2, \ldots, I_K\}$ be the set of interaction types where K is the number of types of interactions. $I_k \in \mathbb{R}^{n \times n}$ denotes the k-th type of interaction, and entities in I_k represent the interaction frequencies. For example, $I_k(i, j)$ is the interaction frequencies between u_i and u_j in the k-th interaction. Therefore, for each pair of users (u_i, u_j), interaction measure is defined as

$$IM(i, j) = \frac{\sum_{k=1}^m I_k(i, j)}{\sum_{\ell=1}^n \sum_{k=1}^m I_k(i, \ell)}; \tag{3.2}$$

the molecular of Eq. (3.2) is the total interaction frequencies between u_i and u_j while the denominator is the total interaction frequency of u_i.

Similarity-based methods can be incorporated into other types of unsupervised methods to improve their performance. For example, rating similarity is exploited to enrich traditional trust propagation methods [11] and it demonstrates that predicting trust is more successful for pairs of users that are similar to each other if we combine the topology of the trust network with rating similarity.

Propagation-based Methods

Propagation-based methods directly capture two properties of trust, i.e., transitivity and comparability. Transitivity allows trust to be propagated to reach other users and comparability denotes that we should aggregate propagating results from multiple paths. One of the earliest propagation framework is proposed in [44]. It suggests four types of atomic propagations, as shown in Figure 3.8: direct propagation, co-citation, transpose trust, and trust coupling as:

- if u_i trusts u_j, and u_j trusts u_k, *direct propagation* allows us to infer that u_i trusts u_k, and its corresponding operator is $\mathbf{T}$;

- *co-citation propagation* says that u_ℓ should trust u_j if u_i trusts u_j and u_k, and u_ℓ trusts u_k. $\mathbf{T}^\top \mathbf{T}$ is the operator of co-citation propagation;

- in *transpose trust*, u_i's trust of u_j causes u_j to develop some level of trust toward u_i, and its operator is $\mathbf{T}^\top$; and

- *trust coupling* suggests that u_i and u_j trust u_k, so trusting u_i should imply trusting u_j. $\mathbf{T}\mathbf{T}^\top$ is its operator.

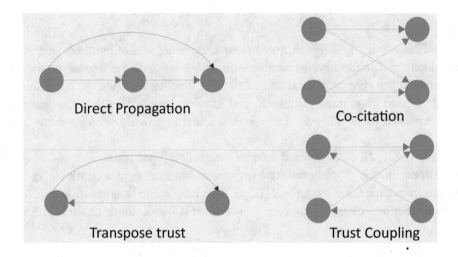

Figure 3.8: Four types of atomic propagations.

$\mathbf{C}$ is defined as a single combined matrix of all four types of atomic propagations,

$$\mathbf{C} = \alpha_1 \mathbf{T} + \alpha_2 \mathbf{T}^\top \mathbf{T} + \alpha_3 \mathbf{T}^\top + \alpha_4 \mathbf{T}\mathbf{T}^\top,$$

where α_1, α_2, α_3, and α_4 control contributions from direct propagation, co-citation, transpose trust and trust coupling, respectively.

Let $\mathbf{C}^k$ be a matrix where $\mathbf{C}^k_{ij}$ denotes the propagation from u_i to u_j after k atomic propagations, and the final matrix representation of the user-user trust relation $\tilde{\mathbf{T}}$ is estimated according to[44],

$$\tilde{\mathbf{T}} = \sum_{k=1}^{K} \gamma^k \mathbf{C}^k,$$

where K is the number of steps of propagation and γ^k is a discount factor to penalize a lengthy path, or a large number of propagation steps.

The original trust propagation algorithm treats all propagation paths equally. However, shorter propagation paths produce more accurate trust estimates and paths with higher trust values create better results [39]. Therefore, a pair of users u_i and u_s without explicit trust relations, a trust value from u_i to u_s is aggregated from suggestions from u_i's trustees to u_s. For those trustees u_i strongly trusts, their suggestions should be weighted more in the aggregation and vise versa; hence each suggestion from u_i's trustee is weighted by how much u_i trusts that trustee. TidalTrust [39] is proposed based on the above intuitions and it is formally defined as:

$$\mathbf{T}_{is} = \frac{\sum_{u_j \in \mathcal{N}_i} \mathbf{T}_{ij} \mathbf{T}_{js}}{\sum_{u_j \in \mathcal{N}_i} \mathbf{T}_{ij}},$$

where $\mathcal{N}_i$ is the set of direct neighbors of u_i. Similar to TidalTrust, MoleTrust also aggregates suggestions from users' trustees [96]. However, MoleTrust removes those cyclic paths in a trust network before the aggregation, which significantly reduces the number of trust propagation paths and increases the efficiency. In general, the propagation process of TidalTrust and MoleTrust is inherited from the idea of random walk. There are also propagation-based methods based on other processes. For example, Advogato is based on maximum network flow process; Appleseed models trust as energy and injects it from the source user to other users along explicit trust relations in the trust network [169]; and trust propagation rules are developed in [123] based on information theoretic frameworks.

Propagation-based methods strongly depend on existing connections (or trust relations) among users. To predict a trust value from a pair of users (u_i, u_j) without a explicit trust relation in a trust network, propagation-based methods need propagation paths from u_i to u_j; hence they may fail to predict trust values for those pairs without any propagation paths or with few propagation paths.

Low-rank Approximation

The low-rank matrix factorization method is widely employed in various applications such as collaborative filtering and document clustering. A few factors can influence the establishment of trust relations and a user usually establishes trust relations with a small proportion of users in a given trust network, resulting in a very sparse and low-rank user-user trust relation matrix $\mathbf{T}$; hence, users can have a more compact but accurate representation in a low-rank space [132]. Let $\mathbf{U} \in \mathbb{R}_+^{n \times d}$, $d \ll n$ be the low-rank representation where $\mathbf{U}_i$ is the low-rank representation of u_i. Trust between u_i and u_j is modeled as the correlation of their low-rank representations as:

$$\mathbf{T}_{ij} = \mathbf{U}_i \mathbf{V} \mathbf{U}_j^\top, \tag{3.3}$$

where $\mathbf{V} \in \mathbb{R}_+^{d \times d}$ captures the correlations among low-rank representations. The trust model in Eq. (3.3) can capture several important properties of trust such as transitivity and asymmetry. For example, if u_i and u_j are highly correlated, and u_j and u_k are highly correlated, it is likely that u_i and u_k are highly correlated; while the learned $\mathbf{V}$ could be asymmetric, therefore $\mathbf{T}_{ij} = \mathbf{U}_i \mathbf{V} \mathbf{U}_j^\top$

could be unequal to $\mathbf{T}_{ji} = \mathbf{U}_j \mathbf{V} \mathbf{U}_i^\top$. The problem of learning low-rank representations of users $\mathbf{U}$ and the correlation matrix $\mathbf{V}$ can be formulated as the standard matrix factorization problem, which sloves the following optimization problem:

$$\min_{\mathbf{U} \geq 0, \mathbf{V} \geq 0} \sum_{i=1}^{n} \sum_{j=1}^{n} (\mathbf{T}_{ij} - \mathbf{U}_i \mathbf{V} \mathbf{U}_j^\top)^2, \qquad (3.4)$$

Eq. (3.4) essentially minimizes the square errors between the observed trust values $\mathbf{T}_{ij}$ and the estimated trust values $\mathbf{U}_i \mathbf{V} \mathbf{U}_j^\top$. To avoid over-fitting, two smoothness regularizations are added on $\mathbf{U}$ and $\mathbf{V}$, respectively, into Eq. (3.4), and then we have,

$$\min_{\mathbf{U} \geq 0, \mathbf{V} \geq 0} \|\mathbf{T} - \mathbf{U} \mathbf{V} \mathbf{U}^\top\|_F^2 + \alpha \|\mathbf{U}\|_F^2 + \beta \|\mathbf{V}\|_F^2, \qquad (3.5)$$

where α and β are non-negative, and are introduced to control the capability of $\mathbf{U}$ and $\mathbf{V}$, respectively. $\|\mathbf{T} - \mathbf{U} \mathbf{V} \mathbf{U}^\top\|_F^2$ is the matrix form of $\sum_{i=1}^{n} \sum_{j=1}^{n} (\mathbf{T}_{ij} - \mathbf{U}_i \mathbf{V} \mathbf{U}_j^\top)^2$ in Eq. (3.4) where $\|\mathbf{X}\|_F$ is the Frobenius norm of the matrix of $\mathbf{X}$ with $\|\mathbf{X}\|_F = \sqrt{\mathbf{X}_{ij}^2}$. After we learn $\mathbf{U}$ and $\mathbf{V}$, the matrix representation of the user-user trust relations $\tilde{\mathbf{T}}$ is estimated as $\tilde{\mathbf{T}} = \mathbf{U} \mathbf{V} \mathbf{U}^\top$ where the estimated trust value from u_i to u_j is suggested by $\tilde{\mathbf{T}}_{ij}$.

The cost of the formation of trust relations in social media is low; hence nodes (or users) of trust networks in social media can have hundreds of trust relations. In other words, trust relations in social media might be noisy. The standard matrix factorization is to minimize the square errors, which is not robust to noise. Huang et al. also consider trust prediction problem as a k-low-rank matrix completion problem [56] but they choose ℓ_1-norm rather than the Frobenius norm (or F-norm) to make the proposed framework robust to noise.

$$\min_{\mathbf{X}} \sum_{(i,j) \in \mathcal{T}} \|\mathbf{X}_{ij} - \mathbf{T}_{ij}\|_1$$
$$s.t.\ rank(\mathbf{X}) \leq k,$$

where $\mathcal{T}$ is the set of pairs of users with observed trust relations and $\mathbf{X}$ is the k low-rank approximation matrix for $\mathbf{T}$ where $\mathbf{X}_{ij}$ is the estimated trust value from u_i to u_j.

In social sciences, it is well known that trust bias is an integrated part in the final trust decision. Trust bias refers to the difficulty of a user to trust others. In reality, some users are easy to trust others, while it is difficult for some users to trust others. Therefore, it would be helpful if we can incorporate trust bias into trust metrics. In [156], a low-rank approximation framework is proposed to capture three types of trust bias including global bias, trustor bias, and trustee bias as follows:

- *Global bias*: It captures the average level of trust for a given community. Global bias is defined based on the observation that in some online sites such as e-commerce, users tend to rate optimiztically while in others, such as security-related applications, users are more conservative.

- *Trustor bias*: In social media, some trustors are more likely to specify higher trust ratings than others. Trustor bias reflects the propensity of a trustor to trust others.

- *Trustee bias*: It is defined to characterize the fact that some trustees are more likely to be trusted than others.

3.3   EVALUATION OF PREDICTING TRUST

Algorithms of predicting trust can be classified differently from different perspectives; hence correspondingly, many evaluation metrics are proposed to assess the performance of algorithms of predicting trust from different perspectives including ranking-based, RMSE, leave-one-out cross-validation and F-measure evaluation. In this section, we first introduce several public available datasets for trust prediction study and then discuss various evaluation metrics.

3.3.1   DATASETS FOR PREDICTING TRUST

Here we introduce several representative datasets for the task of trust prediction as follows:

- *Ciao [133]*: Ciao is a product review site. Users in Ciao can rate products with reviews and they can rate the helpfulness of reviews from other users. In addition, users can explicitly establish trust relations with other users and trust in Ciao is binary. This dataset provides information of trust, item ratings, categories of items, review content, and helpfulness ratings.

- *Epinions [134]*: Epinions is also a product review site. Users can write reviews for items with rating scores from 1–5. They also can rate the helpfulness of reviews and establish binary trust relations with other users. In addition to information provided by the Ciao dataset, the Epinions dataset also provides rich temporal information about the creations of trust relations, item ratings and helpfulness ratings. Another unquietness of the Epinions dataset is that it provides distrust information, which can be used to study the task of incorporating distrust in trust computing.

- *Advogato*:[1] Advogato is an expert site and provides four levels of trust assertions, i.e., "Observer," "Apprentice," "Journeyer," and "Master," to allow its users to certify each other. The degree of trust can be obtained by map those assertions into real numbers; thus, it is different from binary trust in Ciao and Epinions datasets.

- *PGP [46]*: PGP stands for Pretty Good Privacy and it uses " web of trust" to create a decentralized model for data encryption and decryption. Similar to Advogato, PGP also allows its users to specify four levels of trust to other users.

[1]http://www.trustlet.org/wiki/Advogato_dataset.

3.3.2   RANKING-BASED EVALUATION

A typical experimental setting for ranking-based evaluation is illustrated in Figure 3.9. $\mathcal{A} = \{\langle u_i, u_j \rangle | \mathbf{T}_{ij} \neq 0\}$ is the set of pairs of users with trust relations and $\mathcal{B} = \{\langle u_i, u_j \rangle | \mathbf{T}_{ij} = 0\}$ is the set of pairs of users without trust relations. The pairs in $\mathcal{A}$ are sorted in chronological order in terms of the time when they established trust relations. We choose $x\%$ of $\mathcal{A}$ as old trust relations $\mathcal{O}$ and the remaining $1 - x\%$ as new trust relations $\mathcal{N}$ to predict. A trust predictor is trained with old trust relations $\mathcal{O}$. It ranks pairs of users in $\mathcal{N} \cup \mathcal{B}$ by the confidence in a descending order, and chooses top-$|\mathcal{N}|$ ranked pairs as predicted trust relations $\mathcal{C}$. The quality of the predicted trust relations is calculated as:

$$PA = \frac{|\mathcal{N} \cap \mathcal{C}|}{|\mathcal{N}|}.$$

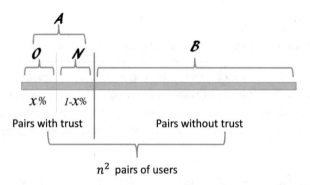

Figure 3.9: Experimental setting for ranking-based evaluation. $\mathcal{A}$ is the set of pairs with trust relations, sorted in chronological order, $x\%$ of which is chosen as old trust relations $\mathcal{O}$ and the remaining $1 - x\%$ as new trust relations $\mathcal{N}$ to predict, and $\mathcal{B}$ is the set of pairs without trust relations. Note that with the increase of x, the PA performance usually decreases.

The value of PA is usually small and to demonstrate the significance of performance, randomly guessing predictor is usually used as a baseline method. Note that with the increase of x, the PA performance reduces. With the increase of x, the size of $\mathcal{N}$ decreases. Since the size of $\mathcal{B}$ is fixed, it becomes more and more difficult to predict $\mathcal{N}$, which is buried in $\mathcal{B}$. Ranking-based evaluation is suitable to assess the performance of algorithms of predicting binary trust in unsupervised scenarios.

3.3.3   RMSE EVALUATION

Similar to the experimental setting for ranking-based evaluation, we often first sort pairs with trust relations in $\mathcal{A}$ in chronological order, then choose $x\%$ of $\mathcal{A}$ as old trust relations $\mathcal{O}$ and the remaining $1 - x\%$ as new trust relations $\mathcal{N}$. A trust predictor will first compute trust values for pairs of users in $\mathcal{N}$, and then RMSE is calculated as:

$$RMSE = \sqrt{\frac{\sum_{(i,j)\in\mathcal{N}}(\hat{\mathbf{T}}_{ij} - \mathbf{T}_{ij})^2}{|\mathcal{N}|}},$$

where $\hat{\mathbf{T}}_{ij}$ is the estimated trust value from u_i to u_j. Although improvement in terms of RMSE is usually very small, small improvement in RMSE can have a significant impact on the quality of trust predictors. RMSE evaluation is widely used to evaluate algorithms of predicting continuous trust in unsupervised scenarios.

3.3.4   LEAVE-ONE-OUT CROSS-VALIDATION EVALUATION

Leave-one-out cross-validation evaluation is to assess how accurately a trust predictor can infer a trust relation by given all other observed trust relations. Formally given a pair (u_i, u_j) in $\mathcal{A}$, the leave-one-out cross-validation evaluation computes the probability of a trust predictor to predict (u_i, u_j) as a new trust relation by leveraging information of other pairs in $\mathcal{A}$. The working of leave-one-out cross-validation evaluation contains following steps:

1. randomly hiding one of the trust relations in $\mathcal{A}$ with replacement;

2. predicting the existence of the hidden trust relation that has been suppressed by using a trust predictor trained with other trust relations; and

3. repeating steps **1** and **2** N times.

If the predictor infers those hidden relations correctly M out of N times, the leave-one-out cross-validation performance is $\frac{M}{N}$. It is easy to verify that leave-one-out cross-validation evaluation of random guessing is 50%. The leave-one-out cross-validation evaluation is widely used to assess the performance of algorithms of predicting binary trust in supervised scenarios.

3.3.5   F-MEASURE EVALUATION

Supervised and binary trust metrics consider trust prediction as a binary classification problem. Consequently, metrics to assess the performance of binary classifiers could be used to evaluate the performance of those trust metrics. Supervised trust metrics consider trust relations as positive samples and missing relations as negative samples. In a typical trust network in social media, the number of negative samples are much larger than that of positive samples, in other words, the class distributions are highly imbalanced. Therefore, only those metrics robust to the imbalance problem can be used to assess the performance of supervised trust metrics, and precision, recall and F-measure are most popular ones. Definitions of precision, recall, and F-measure for binary classifiers are based on the confusion matrix shown in Table 3.1.

Table 3.1: Confusion matrix of a binary classifier

	True class = +1	True class = -1
Predicted class = +1	true pos. (tp)	false pos. (fp)
Predicted class = -1	false neg. (fn)	true neg. (tn)

Based on the confusion matrix, precision and recall are defined as:

$$precision = \frac{tp}{tp + fp}, \quad recall = \frac{tp}{tp + fn}.$$

It is easy to achieve either high precision or high recall. For example, we can obtain 100% recall performance by predicting all pairs as trust relations while we have a very high probability of achieving 100% precision performance by predicting the pair with the highest confidence as a trust relation. F-measure is a tradeoff between precision and recall, which is the harmonic mean of precision and recall. In summary, F-measure evaluation is suitable to assess the performance of supervised and binary trust metrics.

3.4   RECENT ADVANCES IN PREDICTING TRUST

3.4.1   PREDICTING MULTI-DIMENSIONAL TRUST

The majority of existing trust metrics assume single-dimensional and homogeneous trust relations between users. However, trust, as a social concept, has many facets [133], indicating multi-dimensional and heterogeneous trust relations between users. People's multi-faceted interests and experts of different types suggest that people may place trust differently to different people. In [133], multi-dimensional trust is represented as a multi-dimensional matrix or tensor. Let $\mathcal{A} \in \mathbb{R}^{n \times n \times K}$ represent multi-dimensional trust relations among n users in K dimensions. Each element $\mathcal{A}_{ijk}$ indicates the trust relation from u_i to u_j in the k-th dimension. Compared to matrix factorization for single-dimensional trust metrics, tensor factorization is proposed for multi-dimensional trust metrics as:

$$\hat{\mathcal{A}} = \arg \min_{\hat{\mathcal{A}}} \|\mathcal{A} - \hat{\mathcal{A}}\|,$$

where the low-rank tensor $\hat{\mathcal{A}}$ can be expressed as follows:

$$\hat{\mathcal{A}} = \mathcal{C} \times_1 \mathbf{U}^{(1)} \times_2 \mathbf{U}^{(2)} \times_3 \mathbf{U}^{(3)},$$

where $\mathcal{C}$ is the core tensor and can be computed as $\mathcal{C} = \mathcal{A} \times_1 (\mathbf{U}^{(1)})^\top \times_2 (\mathbf{U}^{(2)})^\top \times_3 (\mathbf{U}^{(3)})^\top$. $U^{(1)} \in \mathbb{R}^{n \times r_1}$ consists of the first r_1 columns of $\mathbf{U}_1$ in $\mathbf{D}_1 = \mathbf{U}_1 \Sigma_1 \mathbf{U}_1^\top$ where $\mathbf{D}_1$ is a symmetric and positive semi-definite matrix and its (u, v)-th entry of $\mathbf{D}_1$ is give by,

$$\sum_i \sum_j \mathcal{A}_{uij} \mathcal{A}_{vij},$$

where $\mathcal{A}_{uij}$ and $\mathcal{A}_{vij}$ are elements of the 1st order tensor $\mathcal{A}$. The mode-n product of a tensor $\mathcal{A} \in \mathbb{R}^{I_1 \times I_2 \times \dots \times I_N}$ and a matrix $\mathbf{Q} \in \mathbb{R}^{J_n \times I_n}$ is a tensor, denoted as

$$\mathcal{A} \times_n \mathbf{Q} \in \mathbb{R}^{I_1 \times \dots \times I_{n-1} \times J_n \times I_{n+1} \dots I_N}$$

whose entries are given by

$$(\mathcal{A} \times_n \mathbf{Q})_{i_1, \dots, i_{n-1}, j_n, i_{n+1}, \dots, i_N} = \sum_{i_n} \mathcal{A}_{i_1, \dots, i_{n-1}, i_n, i_{n+1}, \dots, i_N} \mathbf{Q}_{j_n, i_n}.$$

3.4.2   PREDICTING TRUST WITH TEMPORAL DYNAMICS

The vast majority of existing trust metrics assume static trust relationships among users. The assumption may be true for some short time period applications, but it is usually unacceptable for long-running social media application systems. Social media application systems are highly dynamic. Existing dynamics can be categorized into four types: user-related dynamics; content-related dynamics; system-related dynamics; and external event-related dynamics. For example, as time goes on a user's interests may change (user-related dynamics); a product's attraction or freshness may decay (content-related dynamics); and new important products or new influential users may be introduced into the systems (system-related dynamics). Some dynamics may bring short-term change to trust relationships while others may bring long-term impact to trust relations. Therefore, exploiting temporal dynamics can be important to improve the performance of trust prediction and has attracted increasing attention recently. For example, in [13], two unsupervised trust metrics based on matrix factorization are proposed including Temporal Smoothness Matrix Factorization (TSMF) and Temporal Weight Matrix Factorization (TWMF) as follows:

- TSMF introduces a user preference matrix $\mathbf{U}^t$ at each time stamp t and assumes that user preferences change smoothly, which are modeled into the following formulation:

$$\min_{\mathcal{U}, \mathcal{V}} \quad \sum_{t=1}^{m} \|\mathbf{T}_t - \mathbf{U}_t \mathbf{V}_t \mathbf{U}_t^\top\|_F^2 + \alpha \sum_{t=1}^{m} \|\mathbf{V}_t\|_F^2$$
$$+ \beta \sum_{t=1}^{m} \|\mathbf{U}_t\|_F^2 + \gamma \sum_{t=2}^{m} \|\mathbf{U}_t - \mathbf{U}_{t-1}\|_F^2$$
$$s.t. \quad \mathbf{U}_t \geq 0, \quad \mathbf{V}_t \geq 0, \quad t \in [1, m],$$

where $\mathbf{T}_t$ is the adjacency matrix of a trust network at time t, m the number of time stamps, $\mathbf{V}_t$ the correlation matrix at time t. The term $\sum_{t=2}^{m} \|\mathbf{U}_t - \mathbf{U}_{t-1}\|_F^2$ captures the smoothing change assumption (or a Markov assumption) by forcing user preferences at two consecutive time stamps close.

- The earlier trust relations reflect users' previous preferences and should have less influence on the current trust prediction. Assume that the time stamp for u_i creating a trust relation to u_j is g_{ij}^t. TWMF makes use of an exponential time function $e^{-\eta_i(m-g_{ij}^t)}$ to control the importance of the trust relation from u_i to u_j in trust prediction, which is formally defined as:

$$\min_{\mathbf{U},\mathbf{V},\eta_i} \quad \sum_{i=1}^{n}\sum_{j=1}^{n} e^{-\eta_i(m-g_{ij}^t)}\|\mathbf{T}_{ij} - \mathbf{U}_i\mathbf{V}\mathbf{U}_j^\top\|_2^2$$

$$+ \alpha\sum_{i=1}^{n}\|\eta_i\|_2^2 + \beta\|\mathbf{U}\|_F^2 + \gamma\|\mathbf{V}\|_F^2$$

$$s.t. \quad \mathbf{U},\ \mathbf{V} \geq 0,\ \ \eta_i \geq 0,\ \forall\, i \in [1,n].$$

η_i is introduced as a personalized decaying ratio for u_i since users may change their user preferences differently. The importance of $\mathbf{T}_{ij}$ on the learning of the user preference matrix $\mathbf{U}$ and the correlation matrix $\mathbf{V}$ is controlled by $e^{-\eta_i(m-g_{ij}^t)}$.

3.4.3   PREDICTING TRUST WITH SOCIAL THEORIES

Trust metrics, especially unsupervised trust metrics, strongly depend on the connectivities of given trust networks and may suffer from the data sparsity problem since trust networks in social media are usually very sparse. Recently, researchers start exploiting social theories such as homophily [132] and status theory [148] to mitigate the data sparsity problem to improve the performance of trust metrics. Below we use homophily as an example to illustrate how to exploit social theories and why it could mitigate the data sparsity problem.

Homophily is one of the most important theories that explain why people establish trust relations with each other. The homophily effect suggests that similar users have a higher likelihood to establish trust relations. For example, people with similar tastes about items are more likely to trust each other in product review sites. To model homophily, *homophily coefficient* between u_i and u_j, $\zeta(i,j)$, is defined to satisfy: (1) $\zeta(i,j) \in [0,1]$; (2) $\zeta(i,j) = \zeta(j,i)$; and (3) the larger $\zeta(i,j)$ is, the more likely a trust relation is established between u_i and u_j. With homophily coefficient, homophily regularization based on the low-rank trust predictor is introduced as

$$\min \quad \sum_{i=1}^{n}\sum_{j=1}^{n}\zeta(i,j)\|\mathbf{U}_i - \mathbf{U}_j\|_2^2,$$

where users close to each other in the low-rank space are more likely to establish trust relations and their distances in the latent space are controlled by their homophily coefficients. For example, $\zeta(i,j)$ determines the latent distance between u_i and u_j. A larger value of $\zeta(i,j)$ indicates that u_i and u_j are more likely to establish trust relations according to the property (3) of homophily coefficient. Thus we force their latent representations to be as close as possible, while a smaller value of $\zeta(i,j)$ tells that the distance of their latent representations should be larger. For a particular user u_i, the terms in homophily regularization related to his/her latent representation $\mathbf{U}_i$

are,

$$\sum_{j=1}^{n} \zeta(i,j)\|\mathbf{U}_i - \mathbf{U}_j\|_2^2,$$

where the latent representation for u_i is smoothed with other users, controlled by homophily coefficient. Hence, even for long tail users, with a few or even no trust relations, we still can get an approximate estimate of their latent representations via homophily regularization, that mitigates the data sparsity problem in traditional trust metrics.

CHAPTER 4

Applying Trust

Trust provides information about with whom we should share information and from whom we should collect information. Trust has been widely applied in various domains. For example, global trust (or positive reputation) can be used in e-commerce and P2P systems [64] to help online users make decisions; while local trust can help users find relevant and credible information. One essential application of trust is recommendation. Actually, recommendation is one of the most important and successful applications of trust and plays a crucial role in helping online users find relevant and credibility information in social media, which has cultivated a new research field of recommendation, i.e., trust-aware recommender systems [97]. In this chapter, we focus on applying trust in recommendation since recommendation is a quite general task and many other trust-related applications such as information filtering can be essentially considered a recommendation problem.

4.1 TRADITIONAL RECOMMENDER SYSTEMS

Recommender systems became an independent research area in the mid-1990s [2] and have attracted much attention from multiple disciplines, such as mathematics, physics, psychology, and computer science. For example, the winners of the Netflix prize contest, one of the widely known competitions for recommendation, consist of psychologists, computer scientists, and physicists.[1] In a typical recommender system, there are a set of users and a set of items. Let $\mathcal{U} = \{u_1, u_2, \ldots, u_n\}$ and $\mathcal{V} = \{v_1, v_2, \ldots, v_m\}$ be the sets of users and items respectively, where n is the number of users and m is the number of items. A user u_i rates a subset of items with some scores. We use $\mathbf{R} \in \mathbb{R}^{n \times m}$ to denote the user-item rating matrix where $\mathbf{R}_{ij}$ is the rating score if u_i gives a rating to v_j, otherwise we usually employ the symbol "?" to denote the unknown ratings, as shown in Figure 4.1.

Usually the user-item rating matrix is very sparse, suggesting that there are lots of unknown ratings in $\mathbf{R}$. For example, the density of the user-item rating matrix in commercial recommender systems is often less than 1% [119]. The task of recommender systems is to predict the rating for user u_i on a non-rated item v_j or to recommend some items for given users, i.e., to predict missing values in $\mathbf{R}$ based on known ratings. Many techniques are used to build recommender systems, which can be generally classified into content-based, collaborative filtering (CF)-based, and hybrid methods [2].

---

[1]http://en.wikipedia.org/wiki/Netflix_Prize

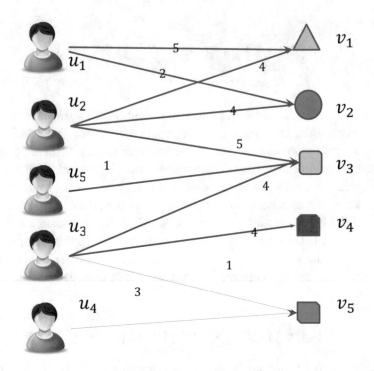

(a) Users Rating Items

	v_1	v_2	v_3	v_4	v_5
u_1	5	2	?	?	?
u_2	4	4	5	?	?
u_3	?	?	4	4	1
u_4	?	?	?	?	3
u_5	?	?	1	?	?

(b) User-item Rating Matrix

Figure 4.1: User-item rating matrix in recommendation. A typical question of recommendation is if user u_1 has ratings for items v_1 and v_2, what are his/her ratings for v_3 to v_5.

4.1.1   CONTENT-BASED RECOMMENDER SYSTEMS

Content-based recommender systems have their roots in information retrieval [7] and information filtering research [9]. They recommend items similar to the ones that the user has preferred in
the past. Most existing content-based recommender systems focus on recommending items with
textual information such as news, books, and documents and are extended to other domains such
as music via deep learning techniques recently. Content-based recommender systems recommend
items to a user which are similar to items the user liked in the past. In particular, various candidate
items are compared with items previously rated by the user. A similarity measure such as a cosine
similarity measure is adopted to score those candidate items. Besides the traditional heuristics
based information retrieval methods, there are also content-based recommender systems that use
other techniques such as various classification and clustering algorithms.

   Content-based recommender systems have several limitations: (1) *limited content analysis*—
those systems are difficult to apply to domains which have an inherent problem with automatic
feature extraction such as multimedia data; (2) *over-specialization*—items recommended to a user
are limited to those similar to items the user already rated; and (3) *new user problem*—to let content
based recommender systems understand a user's preference, the user has to rate a sufficient number
of items, hence content-based recommender systems fail to recommend items for users with few
or no ratings.

4.1.2   COLLABORATIVE FILTERING-BASED RECOMMENDER SYSTEMS

Collaborative filtering (CF) is one of the most popular techniques to build recommender systems [69, 119]. It can predict user interests directly by uncovering complex and unexpected patterns from a user's past behaviors such as product ratings without any domain knowledge. The
underlying assumption of CF-based recommender systems is that if users have agreed with each
other in the past, they are more likely to agree with each other in the future than to agree with randomly chosen users. Existing CF-based methods can be categorized into memory-based methods
and model-based methods.

Memory-based Collaborative Filtering
Memory-based methods use either the whole user-item matrix or a sample to generate a prediction, which can be further divided into user-oriented methods [12] and item-oriented methods [65, 119]. User-oriented methods predict an unknown rating from a user on an item as the
weighted average of all the ratings from her similar users on the item, while item-oriented methods predict the rating from a user on an item based on the average ratings of similar items by the
same user. The key problems a memory-based CF method has to solve are computing similarity and aggregating ratings. Pearson Correlation Coefficient, Cosine similarity, and probability-
based similarity [65] are widely used similarity metrics, and various aggregating strategies have
been discussed in [65]. Next, we use user-oriented methods as examples to illustrate representative
methods for computing similarity and aggregating ratings.

Computing similarity for user-oriented methods: Computing user-user similarity is a critical step for user-oriented methods. There are many techniques proposed to tackle this problem such as Pearson Correlation Coefficient, Cosine similarity, and probability-based similarity, among which Pearson Correlation Coefficient and Cosine similarity are the most widely used ones.

- *Pearson Correlation Coefficient:* Each user is presented as a vector of ratings. For example, the vector of the i-th user is the i-th row of the user-item rating matrix, denoted as $\mathbf{R}_i$. Pearson Correlation Coefficient measures the extent to which two variables linearly relate with each other. Pearson Correlation Coefficient between u_i and u_j can be calculated as

$$\mathbf{S}_{ij} = \frac{\sum_{k \in I}(R_{ik} - \bar{R}_i) \cdot (R_{jk} - \bar{R}_j)}{\sqrt{\sum_{k \in I}(R_{ik} - \bar{R}_i)^2}\sqrt{\sum_{k \in I}(R_{jk} - \bar{R}_j)^2}},$$

where I denotes the set of items rated by both u_i and u_j and $\mathbf{S} \in \mathbb{R}^{n \times n}$ represents the user-user similarity matrix where $\mathbf{S}_{ij}$ is the similarity between u_i and u_j. Note that the value of $\mathbf{S}_{ij}$ is between -1 and 1; hence, we usually adopt a function to map $\mathbf{S}_{ij}$ to $[0, 1]$. $\bar{R}_i$ denotes the average rate of u_i.

- *Cosine similarity:* Cosine similarity computes the cosine of the angle formed by the rating vectors. For example, the cosine similarity between u_i and u_j can be calculated as

$$\mathbf{S}_{ij} = \frac{\sum_{k \in I} R_{ik} \cdot R_{jk}}{\sqrt{\sum_{k \in I} R_{ik}^2}\sqrt{\sum_k R_{jk}^2}}.$$

Aggregating ratings for user-oriented methods: After obtaining a user-user similarity matrix, user-oriented methods predict a missing rating for a given user by aggregating the ratings of users similar to her. Below are some widely used ones.

- *Average Rating Aggregation:* the predicted rating from u_i to v_j is the average aggregation of ratings to v_j from u_i's top-K most similar users $\mathcal{N}_i$ as:

$$\hat{\mathbf{R}}_{ij} = \frac{1}{|\mathcal{N}_i|} \sum_{u_k \in \mathcal{N}_i} \mathbf{R}_{kj},$$

- *Weighted Average Rating Aggregation:* It weights the ratings from users in $\mathcal{N}_i$ by the similarities between u_i and users in $\mathcal{N}_i$ as:

$$\hat{\mathbf{R}}_{ij} = \frac{\sum_{u_k \in \mathcal{N}_i} \mathbf{S}_{ik}\mathbf{R}_{kj}}{\sum_{u_k \in \mathcal{N}_i} \mathbf{S}_{ik}}.$$

- *Biased Weighted Average Rating Aggregation:* Ratings might have biases. For example, on average, some users tend to give higher ratings than others. Therefore *Biased Weighted Average Rating Aggregation* is a variant of *Weighted Average Rating Aggregation* while considering users' biases as:

$$\hat{\mathbf{R}}_{ij} = \bar{\mathbf{R}}_i + \frac{\sum_{u_k \in \mathcal{N}_i} \mathbf{S}_{ik}(\mathbf{R}_{kj} - \bar{\mathbf{R}}_k)}{\sum_{u_k \in \mathcal{N}_i} \mathbf{S}_{ik}}.$$

Model-based Collaborative Filtering

Model-based methods assume a model to generate the ratings and apply data mining and machine learning techniques to find patterns from training data [157], which can be used to make predictions for unknown ratings. Compared to memory-based CF, model-based CF has a more holistic goal to uncover latent factors that explain observed ratings [157]. Well-known model-based methods include Bayesian belief net CF models [12], clustering CF models [143], random-walk-based methods [57], and factorization-based CF models [69]. Factorization-based CF methods [69, 118] are very competitive if not the best and are widely adopted to build recommender systems. Factorization-based CF models assume that a few latent patterns influence user rating behaviors and perform a low-rank matrix factorization on the user-item rating matrix. Let $\mathbf{U}_i \in \mathbb{R}^K$ and $\mathbf{V}_j \in \mathbb{R}^K$ be the user preference vector for u_i and item characteristic vector for v_j respectively, where K is the number of latent factors. Factorization-based collaborative filtering models solve the following problem

$$\min_{\mathbf{U},\mathbf{V}} \sum_{i=1}^{n} \sum_{j=1}^{m} \mathbf{W}_{ij}(\mathbf{R}_{ij} - \mathbf{U}_i \mathbf{V}_j^{\top})^2 + \alpha(\|\mathbf{U}\|_F^2 + \|\mathbf{V}\|_F^2),$$

where $\mathbf{U} = [\mathbf{U}_1^{\top}, \mathbf{U}_2^{\top}, \ldots, \mathbf{U}_n^{\top}]^{\top} \in \mathbb{R}^{n \times k}$ and $\mathbf{V} = [\mathbf{V}_1^{\top}, \mathbf{V}_2^{\top}, \ldots, \mathbf{V}_m^{\top}]^{\top} \in \mathbb{R}^{m \times K}$. The term $\alpha(\|\mathbf{U}\|_F^2 + \|\mathbf{V}\|_F^2)$ is introduced to avoid over-fitting, controlled by the parameter α. $\mathbf{W} \in \mathbb{R}^{n \times m}$ is a weight matrix where $\mathbf{W}_{ij}$ is the weight for the rating for u_i to v_j. A common way to set $\mathbf{W}$ is $\mathbf{W}_{ij} = 1$ if $\mathbf{R}_{ij} \neq$ "?"; and $\mathbf{W}_{ij} = 0$ if $\mathbf{R}_{ij} =$ "?". The weight matrix $\mathbf{W}$ can also be used to handle the implicit feedback and encode side information such as user click behaviors [34], similarity between users and items [82], quality of reviews [114], and global trust [136].

Discussions

CF-based recommender systems can overcome some of the shortcomings of content-based recommender systems. For example, CF-based systems use rating information; hence, they are domain-independent and can recommend any items. However, CF-based methods have their own limitations including the cold-start problem (new items or new users) and the data sparsity problem.

4.1.3   HYBRID RECOMMENDER SYSTEMS

To avoid certain limitations of content and collaborative filtering systems, hybrid approaches combine content- and CF-based methods. Various strategies are proposed to combine content- and CF-based methods, which can be roughly classified into three categories [2].

- **Combining different recommenders:** Content- and CF-based methods are first implemented separately and their predictions are then combined to obtain the final recommendation. Various ways of combining predictions from content- and CF-based methods are proposed such as a voting scheme and a linear combination of ratings.

- **Adding content-based characteristics to CF-based models:** Systems with this strategy use content-based profiles and uncommonly rated items to calculate user-user similarities. These systems can overcome some data sparsity problems of CF-based methods and recommend items directly when item scores highly against the user's profiles.

- **Adding CF-based characteristics to content-based models:** The most popular approach under this strategy is to use a dimensionality reduction technique on the content profile matrix. For example, latent semantic indexing is used to create a collaborative view of a set of user profiles, which improves recommendation performance compared to pure content-based approaches.

4.2   TRUST-AWARE RECOMMENDER SYSTEMS

In the physical world, people seek recommendations from their trusted friends and are more likely to accept recommendations made by their trusted friends than recommendations from strangers; in other words, trust has potentials in helping the performance improvement of traditional recommender systems. Trust-aware recommender systems have been introduced to exploit the power of trust information to enhance recommender systems.

4.2.1   PROBLEM STATEMENT

Trust-aware recommender systems investigate how to combine trust and rating information for recommendation. Let $\mathbf{T} \in \mathbb{R}^{n \times n}$ denote user-user trust relations where $\mathbf{T}_{ij}$ is the trust strength from u_i to u_j. In addition to rating information $\mathbf{R}$, trust-aware recommender systems can also make use of trust information $\mathbf{T}$ as shown in Figure 4.2, which is formally stated as: *given observed ratings in* $\mathbf{R}$ *and trust information* $\mathbf{T}$, *trust-aware recommendation aims to predict missing ratings in* $\mathbf{R}$ *by leveraging both observed ratings in* $\mathbf{R}$ *and trust information* $\mathbf{T}$.

4.2.2   OPPORTUNITIES FROM TRUST INFORMATION

In a typical recommender system, the user-item matrix is often extremely sparse with less than 1% observed ratings and the vast majority of existing recommender systems suffer from this data

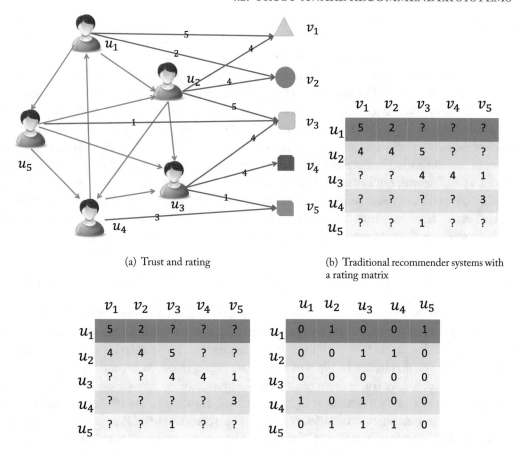

(a) Trust and rating

(b) Traditional recommender systems with a rating matrix

(c) Trust-aware recommender systems with rating and trust matrices

Figure 4.2: Trust-aware recommender systems.

sparsity problem. The number of ratings for users alway follows a power-law-like distribution—a few users with many ratings while most users with few ratings. Furthermore, new users join the recommender systems. Therefore, there are many users with no or very few ratings and existing recommender systems may fail to make recommendations for those so-called cold-start users. Trust information provides opportunities to mitigate the data sparsity and cold-start problems in traditional recommender systems.

First, user-oriented recommender systems suggest items to users by aggregating recommendations from their similar users. In real-world datasets, the overlap between one user's similar users and his/her trusted users is less than 10% [131], which suggests that trust information provides an independent source for recommendation and research findings from trust computing such as trust metrics introduced in Chapter 3 can be applied to build trust-aware recommender systems. Therefore, trust information is complementary to rating information and can mitigate the data-sparsity problem in recommendation.

Second, similar users are likely to trust each other; while users are likely to be influenced by their trusted users and become increasingly similar with their trusted users [132], which can be explained by social correlation theories such as homophily and social influence. One derived conclusion is that users with trust relations are likely to share similar preferences in item ratings. Furthermore, trust information provides unique context, i.e., familiarity, which is also very importance in recommendation since in the physical world, we also ask for suggestions from our friends who are familiar with our tastes [45]. For users with a few or even no ratings, based on their trust relations, we still can make recommendations with similarity and familiarity evidence from their trusted users. Therefore, trust information can significantly reduce the number of cold-start users and can mitigate the cold-start problem in traditional recommender systems.

4.3   EXISTING TRUST-AWARE RECOMMENDER SYSTEMS

Collaborative filtering (CF) is one of the most popular techniques to build recommender systems, and the majority of existing trust-aware recommender systems are built based on CF techniques. Therefore, our discussion focuses on CF-based trust-aware recommender systems. Trust-aware recommender systems have two types of input, i.e., rating information and trust information, as shown in Figure 4.2. A trust-aware recommender system often first chooses a CF-based model as its base model and then extends it to capture trust information. Therefore, a typical CF-based trust-aware recommendation framework contains two components: (1) a base CF model and (2) a trust model. Therefore, the basic CF model paves a way to classify trust-aware recommender systems. Following the way CF-based recommender systems categorized, we classify trust-aware recommender systems into two major categories according to their base CF models: memory-based and model-based trust-aware recommender systems.

4.3.1   MEMORY-BASED TRUST-AWARE RECOMMENDER SYSTEMS

Memory-based trust-aware recommender systems use memory-based CF models, especially user-oriented methods, as their base models. A missing rating for a given user is aggregated from the ratings of his/her correlated users, that are denoted as N^+. For a given user, traditional user-oriented methods use similar users, while memory-based trust-aware recommender systems use correlated users N^+ obtained based on both trust and rating information. Trust-aware recommender systems in this category usually consist of two steps. First, they obtain the correlated users $N^+(i)$ for a given user u_i, and second is the classical last step of memory-based CF methods—aggregating ratings from the correlated users obtained by the first step to predict missing ratings. Trust-aware recommender systems in this category use different approaches to obtain correlated users N^+ in the first step; next, we introduce details about some representative approaches.

Trusted Users

For a given u_i, this strategy simply considers u_i's directly trusted users $\mathcal{F}(i)$ as the set of his/her correlated users $N^+(i)$ [146],

$$N^+(i) = \{u_j | \mathbf{T}_{ij} = 1\}.$$

TidalTrust

This trust-aware recommender system [37] estimates trust values among users based on the following two observations: (1) shorter propagation paths produce more accurate trust estimates; and (2) paths with higher trust values create better results. To estimate trust values among users, TidalTrust performs the following.

- Searching a shortest path from the source user to raters and setting the shortest path length as the path depth of the algorithm.

- Computing trust value from the source user to a rater at the given depth. For a pair of users u_i and u_k who are not directly connected, a trust value is aggregated from the trust value from u_i's direct neighbors to u_j, weighted by the direct trust values from u_i to his/her direct neighbors as

$$\hat{\mathbf{T}}_{ij} = \frac{\sum_{u_k \in \mathcal{F}_i} \hat{\mathbf{T}}_{ik} \hat{\mathbf{T}}_{kj}}{\sum_{u_k \in \mathcal{F}_i} \hat{\mathbf{T}}_{ik}},$$

where $\mathcal{F}_i$ is the set of trustees of u_i and $\hat{\mathbf{T}}_{ij}$ is the estimated trust value from u_i to u_j.

- After trust values in $\hat{\mathbf{T}}$ are calculated, $N^+(i)$ is defined as the set of users whose trust values with u_i exceeds a given threshold τ,

$$N^+(i) = \{u_j | \hat{\mathbf{T}}_{ij} \geq \tau\}.$$

MoleTrust

MoleTrust [98] consists of two major steps. First, cycles in trust networks are removed. To obtain trust values, a large number of trust propagations have to be executed. Therefore, removing trust cycles beforehand from trust networks can significantly speed up the proposed algorithm because every user only needs to be visited once to infer trust values. With this operation, the original trust network is transformed into a directed acyclic graph. Second, trust values are calculated based on the obtained directed acyclic graph by performing a simple graph random walk: the trust of the users at 1-hop away is computed, then the trust of the users at 2-hop away, etc. After trust values are computed, MoleTrust defines users, who are within *maximum-depth* and have rated the target item v_k, as correlated users N^+ as:

$$N^+(i) = \{u_j | \ell_{ij} \leq maximum\text{-}depth \wedge \mathbf{R}_{jk} \neq \text{``?''}\},$$

where ℓ_{ij} is the length of the shortest path from u_i to u_j in the original trust network and *maximum-depth* is a predefined parameter.

Although MoleTrust has similar operations to TidalTrust, they are different in two aspects. First, the definitions of correlated users in these two systems are different. TidalTrust adds a user u_k to $N^+(i)$ only if she is on a shortest path from u_i, while MoleTrust considers all users who have rated the target item and that can be reached through a direct or propagated trust relation within *maximum-depth* as $N^+(i)$. Second, MoleTrust needs a predefined trust threshold to determine users who will be considered in the rating aggregating process, while TidalTrust determines the trust threshold automatically, i.e., the path strength (the minimum trust rating on a path). TidalTrust only considers users in the shortest paths; therefore it is very efficient and it makes recommendations with high precision but low recall. While MoleTrust considers all users within a predefined parameter *maximum-depth* and it makes tradeoff between precision and recall.

TrustWalker

The intuition of this system is from two key observations. One is that a user's trust network has little overlap with his/her similar users and trust information provides an independent source of information. The other observation is that ratings from strongly trusted friends on similar items are more reliable than ratings from weakly trusted neighbors on the same target item. The first observation indicates the importance of trust-based approaches while the second observation suggests the capability of item-oriented approaches. To take advantage of both approaches, TrustWalker proposes a random walk model to combine trust-based and item-oriented approaches into a coherent framework [58]. It queries a user's direct and indirect trusted users' ratings for the target item as well as similar items by performing random walks in the trust networks. Next, we illustrate how TrustWalker obtains a rating from u_i to v_j.

Each random walk returns a rating of v_j and it performs multiple random walks. The final rating from u_i to v_j is calculated by aggregating results of all performed random walks. Each random walk starts from the target user u_i to seek a rating score for v_j. Suppose that we are at a certain node u_v in step k. Then TrustWalker works as follows.

- If u_v has rated v_j, it returns $\mathbf{R}_{vj}$ as the random walk result.

- With the probability ϕ_{vik}, it stops the random walk, selects an item v_ℓ that is similar to v_j, and returns $\mathbf{R}_{v\ell}$ as the random walk result.

- With the probability $1 - \phi_{vik}$, it continues the random walk to a director neighbor of u_v.

TrustWalker employs the Pearson Correlation Coefficient of ratings expressed for items to calculate item-item similarity. Since values of Pearson Correlation Coefficient are in the range of $[-1, 1]$, only items that are positively correlated with the target item are considered. The similarity between v_j and v_ℓ is computed as

$$sim(v_j, v_\ell) = \frac{1}{1 + e^{-\frac{N_{j\ell}}{2}}} \times PCC(v_i, v_\ell),$$

where $N_{j\ell}$ is the number of users who rated both v_j and v_ℓ, and $PCC(j, \ell)$ is Pearson Correlation Coefficient of v_j and v_ℓ.

4.3.2 MODEL-BASED TRUST-AWARE RECOMMENDER SYSTEMS

Model-based trust-aware recommender systems choose model-based CF methods as their base models. Matrix factorization techniques are one of the most popular model-based CF methods. There are several nice properties of these matrix factorization techniques [33]: (1) many optimization methods such as gradient based methods can be applied to find an optimal solution, scalable to thousands of users with millions of trust relations; (2) matrix factorization has a nice probabilistic interpretation with Gaussian noise; and (3) it is very flexible and allows us to include various types of prior knowledge. Most existing trust-aware recommender systems in this category are based on matrix factorization [137]. The common rationale behind these methods is that users' preferences are similar to or influenced by users they trust. However, the low cost of online trust relation formation can lead to trust relations with heterogeneous strengths (e.g., weak trust and strong trust mixed together) [149]. Since users with strong trust are more likely to share similar tastes than those with weak trust, treating all trust relations equally is likely to lead to the degradation of recommendation performance. Therefore, for each trust relation, those methods are associated with a strength, which is usually calculated by rating similarity in existing trust-aware recommender systems. For example, when we choose cosine similarity, if u_i trusts u_k, $\mathbf{S}_{ik}$ is calculated as the cosine similarity between the rating vectors of u_i and u_k, otherwise we set $\mathbf{S}_{ik}$ to 0. Therefore, the strength between u_i and u_k $\mathbf{S}_{ik}$ can be formally defined as:

$$\mathbf{S}_{ik} = \begin{cases} \dfrac{\sum_j \mathbf{R}_{ij} \cdot \mathbf{R}_{kj}}{\sqrt{\sum_j \mathbf{R}_{ij}^2} \sqrt{\sum_j \mathbf{R}_{kj}^2}} & \text{when } u_i \text{ trusts } u_k, \\ 0 & \text{otherwise.} \end{cases}$$

Unlike traditional matrix factorization-based recommender systems, trust-aware recommender systems in this category can take advantage of trust information, and a unified framework can be stated as

$$\min_{\mathbf{U},\mathbf{V},\Omega} \|\mathbf{W} \odot (\mathbf{R} - \mathbf{U}^\top \mathbf{V})\|_F^2 + \alpha \ Trust(\mathbf{T}, \mathbf{S}, \Omega)$$
$$+ \lambda(\|\mathbf{U}\|_F^2 + \|\mathbf{V}\|_F^2 + \|\Omega\|_F^2),$$

where $Trust(\mathbf{T}, \mathbf{S}, \Omega)$ is the trust model introduced to capture trust information and Ω is the set of parameters learned from trust information. α is employed to control the contributions from trust information. $\mathbf{W}$ controls the weights of known ratings in the learning process. According to different definitions of $Trust(\mathbf{T}, \mathbf{S}, \Omega)$, we further divide trust-aware recommender systems in this category into three groups: co-factorization methods, ensemble methods, and regularization methods. Next, we will review some representative systems in detail for each group.

Co-factorization Methods

The underlying assumption of systems in this group is that the i-th user u_i should share the same user preference vector $\mathbf{U}_i$ in the rating space (rating information) and the trust space (trust information). Trust-aware recommender systems in this group perform a co-factorization in the user-item rating matrix $\mathbf{R}$ and the user-user trust relation matrix $\mathbf{T}$ by sharing the same user preference latent factor. SoRec [89] and LOCABAL [136] are two representative systems in this group.

SoRec [89]: It defines $Trust(\mathbf{T}, \mathbf{S}, \Omega)$ as

$$\min \sum_{i=1}^{n} \sum_{u_k \in \mathcal{F}_i} (\mathbf{S}_{ik} - \mathbf{U}_i^\top \mathbf{Z}_k)^2,$$

where $\mathcal{F}_i$ is the set of users trusted by u_i and $\mathbf{Z} = \{\mathbf{Z}_1, \mathbf{Z}_2, \ldots, \mathbf{Z}_n\} \in \mathbb{R}^{K \times n}$ is the factor-specific latent feature matrix. With this term, the user preference matrix $\mathbf{U}$ is learned from both rating information and trust information by solving the following optimization problem:

$$\min_{\mathbf{U}, \mathbf{V}, \mathbf{Z}} \|\mathbf{W} \odot (\mathbf{R} - \mathbf{U}^\top \mathbf{V})\|_F^2 + \alpha \sum_{i=1}^{n} \sum_{u_k \in \mathcal{F}_i} (\mathbf{S}_{ik} - \mathbf{U}_i^\top \mathbf{Z}_k)^2$$
$$+ \lambda(\|\mathbf{U}\|_F^2 + \|\mathbf{V}\|_F^2 + \|\mathbf{Z}\|_F^2),$$

where $\odot$ is the Hadamard product where $(A \odot B)_{ij} = \mathbf{A}_{ij} \mathbf{B}_{ij}$ for any two matrices $\mathbf{A}$ and $\mathbf{B}$ with the same size.

LOCABAL [136]: It defines $Trust(\mathbf{T}, \mathbf{S}, \Omega)$ as

$$\min \sum_{i=1}^{n} \sum_{u_k \in \mathcal{F}_i} (\mathbf{S}_{ik} - \mathbf{U}_i^\top \mathbf{H} \mathbf{U}_k)^2. \tag{4.1}$$

LOCABAL is different from SoRec and it is based on social correlation theories where the user preferences of two users with trust relations are correlated via the correlation matrix $\mathbf{H}$. In Eq. (4.1), for two users u_i and u_k with trust relations, their preference vectors $\mathbf{u}_i$ and $\mathbf{u}_k$ are correlated through $\mathbf{H}$, which is controlled by the trust strength $\mathbf{S}_{ik}$ where $\mathbf{H} \in \mathbb{R}^{K \times K}$ is the matrix to capture the user preference correlation. A large value of $\mathbf{S}_{ik}$, i.e., u_i and u_k with strong trust, indicates that their preferences $\mathbf{u}_i$ and $\mathbf{u}_k$ should be tightly correlated via $\mathbf{H}$, while a small value of $\mathbf{S}_{ik}$ indicates that $\mathbf{u}_i$ and $\mathbf{u}_k$ should be loosely correlated.

With the definition of $Trust(\mathbf{T}, \mathbf{S}, \Omega)$, LOCABAL solves the following optimization problem,

$$\min_{\mathbf{U},\mathbf{V},\mathbf{Z}} \|\mathbf{W} \odot (\mathbf{R} - \mathbf{U}^\top \mathbf{V})\|_F^2 + \alpha \sum_{i=1}^{n} \sum_{u_k \in \mathcal{F}_i} (\mathbf{S}_{ik} - \mathbf{U}_i^\top \mathbf{H} \mathbf{U}_k)^2$$
$$+ \lambda(\|\mathbf{U}\|_F^2 + \|\mathbf{V}\|_F^2 + \|\mathbf{H}\|_F^2).$$

Note that LOCABAL and SeRoc have the same form by further factorizing $\mathbf{z}_k$ into $\mathbf{H}\mathbf{u}_k$. After obtaining factorized factors of the matrix $\mathbf{S}$, we can use the factors to reconstruct $\mathbf{S}$. For LOCABAL, after learning $\mathbf{U}$ and $\mathbf{H}$, we can reconstruct $\mathbf{S}$ as $\hat{\mathbf{S}} = \mathbf{U}^\top \mathbf{H} \mathbf{U}$ and the reconstructed matrix $\hat{\mathbf{S}}$ can be used to perform trust prediction. For example, the trust value from u_i to u_j can be suggested by $\hat{\mathbf{S}}_{ij}$. Hence, co-factorization methods can perform recommendation and trust prediction simultaneously.

Ensemble Methods

The basic idea of ensemble methods is that users and their trust networks should have similar ratings on items, and a missing rating for a given user could be indicated by both his/her own preference or his/her trusted users. Therefore, ensemble methods infer a unknown rating for a user via a linear combination of ratings from the user and his/her trusted users. We give details about two representative systems below.

STE [87]: The rating from the i-th user u_i to the j-th item v_j is estimated by STE as

$$\hat{\mathbf{R}}_{ij} = \mathbf{u}_i^\top \mathbf{v}_j + \beta \sum_{u_k \in \mathcal{F}_i} \mathbf{S}_{ik} \mathbf{U}_k^\top \mathbf{V}_j, \tag{4.2}$$

where $\sum_{u_k \in \mathcal{N}_i} \mathbf{S}_{ik} \mathbf{U}_k^\top \mathbf{V}_j$ is a weighted sum of the predicted ratings for v_j from u_i's trust network, and β controls the influence from trust information. It is easy to verify that Eq. (4.2) is equivalent to the following matrix form:

$$\hat{\mathbf{R}} = (I + \beta \mathbf{S}) \mathbf{U}^\top \mathbf{V}.$$

STE is to minimize the following term:

$$\min_{\mathbf{U},\mathbf{V}} \|\mathbf{W} \odot ((\mathbf{R} - \mathbf{U}^\top \mathbf{V}) - \beta \mathbf{S} \mathbf{U}^\top \mathbf{V}))\|_F^2 + \lambda(\|\mathbf{U}\|_F^2 + \|\mathbf{V}\|_F^2).$$

mTrust [133]: It predicts the rating from u_i to v_j as

$$\hat{\mathbf{R}}_{ij} = \mathbf{u}_i^\top \mathbf{v}_j + \beta \frac{\sum_{u_k \in \mathcal{F}_i} \mathbf{S}_{ik} \mathbf{R}_{kj}}{\sum_{u_k \in \mathcal{F}_i} \mathbf{S}_{ik}},$$

where $\frac{\sum_{u_k \in \mathcal{N}_i} S_{ik} R_{kj}}{\sum_{u_k \in \mathcal{N}_i} S_{ik}}$ is a weighted mean of the ratings for v_j from u_i's trust network. mTrust solves the following optimization problem:

$$\min_{\mathbf{U},\mathbf{V},\mathbf{S}} \sum_i \sum_j (\mathbf{R}_{ij} - \mathbf{u}_i^\top \mathbf{v}_j - \beta \frac{\sum_{u_k \in \mathcal{N}_i} S_{ik} \mathbf{R}_{kj}}{\sum_{u_k \in \mathcal{N}_i} S_{ik}})^2 + \lambda(\|\mathbf{U}\|_F^2 + \|\mathbf{V}\|_F^2).$$

Note that there are two major differences between STE and mTrust. First, $\mathbf{S}_{ik}$ denotes the influence from u_k to u_i for mTrust and will be learned from the data automatically, while $\mathbf{S}_{ik}$ in STE is the predefined similarity between u_i and u_k. Second, STE incorporates a weighted sum of the predicted ratings from trust networks, while mTrust incorporates a weighted mean of the existing ratings from trust networks.

Regularization Methods

Regularization methods focus on a user's preference that is denoted by the user latent factor such as $\mathbf{U}_i$ for the user u_i. They assume that a user's preference should be similar to that of his/her trust network. For a given user u_i, regularization methods generally force his/her preference $\mathbf{U}_i$ to be closer to that of users in u_i's trust network $\mathcal{F}_i$. SocialMF [59] and Social Regularization [90] are two representative systems in this group.

SocialMF [59]: SocialMF forces the preference of a user to be closer to the average preference of the user's trust network and defines $Trust(\mathbf{T}, \mathbf{S}, \Omega)$ as

$$\min \sum_{i=1}^n (\mathbf{U}_i - \sum_{u_k \in \mathcal{F}_i} \mathbf{S}_{ik} \mathbf{U}_k)^2,$$

where $\sum_{u_k \in \mathcal{F}_i} \mathbf{S}_{ik} \mathbf{U}_k$ is the weighted average preference of users in u_i's trust network $\mathcal{N}_i$ and SocialMF requires each row of $\mathbf{S}$ to be normalized to 1. The authors demonstrated that SocialMF addresses the transitivity of trust in trust networks because a user's latent feature vector is dependent on the direct neighbors' latent feature vectors, which can propagate through the network and make a user's latent feature vector dependent on all users in the network.

With the term to capture social information, SocialMF solves the following optimization problem:

$$\min_{\mathbf{U},\mathbf{V}} \|\mathbf{W} \odot (\mathbf{R} - \mathbf{U}^\top \mathbf{V})\|_F^2 + \alpha \sum_{i=1}^n (\mathbf{U}_i - \sum_{u_k \in \mathcal{F}_i} \mathbf{S}_{ik} \mathbf{U}_k)^2 + \lambda(\|\mathbf{U}\|_F^2 + \|\mathbf{V}\|_F^2).$$

Social Regularization [90]: For a given user, users in his/her trust network may have diverse tastes. Incorporating this intuition, social regularization proposes a pair-wise regularization as,

$$\min \sum_{i=1}^n \sum_{u_k \in \mathcal{F}_i} \mathbf{S}_{ik} (\mathbf{U}_i - \mathbf{U}_k)^2,$$

where the preference closeness of two connected users is controlled by their similarity based on their previous ratings. Similarity can be calculated by Pearson Correlation Coefficient or Cosine similarity of commonly rated items by two users with trust relations. A small value of S_{ik} indicates that the distance between latent feature vectors U_i and U_k should be larger, while a large value indicates that the distance between the latent feature vectors should be smaller.

Recommender systems with social regularization solve the following problem:

$$\min_{\mathbf{U},\mathbf{V}} \|\mathbf{W} \odot (\mathbf{R} - \mathbf{U}^\top \mathbf{V})\|_F^2 + \alpha \sum_{i=1}^{n} \sum_{u_k \in \mathcal{F}_i} \mathbf{S}_{ik}(\mathbf{U}_i - \mathbf{U}_k)^2 + \lambda(\|\mathbf{U}\|_F^2 + \|\mathbf{V}\|_F^2).$$

The number of the regularization terms of SocialMF is equal to the number of users in the trust network while that of *Social Regularization* is the number of trust links in the trust network. For a typical trust network in social media, the number of links is usually much larger than that of users; hence, SocialMF has less number of regularization terms and it is computationally efficient. However, it uses the average preference of one's trust network while ignores the fact that users in one's trust network may have diverse tastes; therefore empirical findings that *Social Regularization* is usually more effective than SocialMF. One advantage of regularization based approaches is that they indirectly model the propagation of user preferences in trust networks, which can be used to reduce cold-start users and significantly increase the coverage of items for recommendation.

4.4   PERFORMANCE EVALUATION

In this section, we focus on available datasets and metrics for the evaluation of trust-aware recommender systems.

4.4.1   DATASETS

There are benchmark datasets to evaluate traditional recommender systems such as Netflix data[2] and MovieLens data.[3] Compared to traditional recommendation, there are no agreed benchmark datasets for trust-aware recommender systems. However, there are datasets publicly available for the purpose of research. Below is a list of representative datasets for trust-aware recommender systems.

Epinions03:[4] This dataset was collected by Paolo Massa in a 5-week crawl (November/December 2003) from the Epinions.com [97]. In Epinions, people can write reviews for various products with ratings, and also they can add members to their trust networks or "Circle of Trust." This dataset provides user-item rating information and user-user trust networks. Note that the trust network here is directed.

---

[2]http://en.wikipedia.org/wiki/Netflix_Prize
[3]http://www.grouplens.org/node/73
[4]http://www.trustlet.org/wiki/Downloaded_Epinions_dataset

Ciao:[5] This dataset was collected by authors in Tang et al. [133, 134]. Ciao is a product review website where users can rate and write reviews for various products, and they can also establish trust relations with others. In addition to rating and social information, Ciao provides extra contextual information including temporal information about when ratings are provided, the category information of products, and information about the reviews such as the content and helpfulness votes.

Epinions11:[6] This dataset was collected during 2011 and is also from Epinions [134, 135]. In addition to information in Epinion03, this dataset includes richer information for trust-award recommendation, including temporal information for both rating and trust information, categories of products, information about reviews, and distrust information, which allows advanced research about trust-aware recommendation. For example, the temporal information about when users establish trust relations can be used to study the evolution of trust relations for recommendation; and distrust information allows us to investigate the role of distrust in trust-aware recommender systems.

4.4.2　EVALUATION METRICS

Although the types of input of traditional recommendation and trust-aware recommendation are different, the types of their output are the same, i.e., the predicted values for unknown ratings. Therefore, metrics that evaluate traditional recommender systems can also be applied to evaluate trust-aware recommender systems. To evaluate recommender systems, the data is usually divided into two parts: the training set $\mathcal{K}$ and the testing set $\mathcal{U}$. Recommender systems will be trained based on $\mathcal{K}$, and the quality of recommendation will be evaluated in $\mathcal{U}$. Different evaluation metrics are proposed to assess the quality of recommendation from different perspectives, such as prediction accuracy, ranking accuracy, diversity and novelty, and coverage. Therefore how to choose metrics to evaluate a recommender system strongly depends on the goals the system is designed to fulfill.

Prediction Accuracy

Prediction accuracy measures the closeness of predicted ratings to the true ratings. Two widely used metrics in this category are Mean Absolute Error (MAE) and Root Mean Squared Error (RMSE).

The metric RMSE is defined as

$$RMSE = \sqrt{\frac{\sum_{(u_i, v_j) \in \mathcal{U}} (\mathbf{R}_{ij} - \hat{\mathbf{R}}_{ij})^2}{|\mathcal{U}|}},$$

where $|\mathcal{U}|$ is the size of $\mathcal{U}$ and $\hat{\mathbf{R}}_{ij}$ is the predicted rating from u_i to v_j.

[5]http://www.public.asu.edu/~jtang20/datasetcode/truststudy.htm
[6]http://www.public.asu.edu/~jtang20/datasetcode/truststudy.htm

The metric MAE is defined as

$$MAE = \frac{1}{|\mathcal{U}|} \sum_{(u_i, v_j) \in \mathcal{U}} |\mathbf{R}_{ij} - \hat{\mathbf{R}}_{ij}|.$$

A smaller RMSE or MAE value means better performance, and due to their simplicity, RMSE and MAE are widely used in the evaluation of recommender systems. Note that previous work demonstrated that *small improvement in RMSE or MAE terms can have a significant impact on the quality of the top-few recommendation* [69].

Ranking Accuracy

Ranking accuracy evaluates how many recommended items are purchased by the user. Precision and recall are two popular metrics in this category. Recall captures how many of the acquired items are recommended, while precision captures how many recommended items are acquired; for example, Precision@N is used to indicate how many top-N recommended items are acquired while Recall@N denotes how many top-N acquired items are recommended, which are formally defined as:

$$precision@N = \frac{\sum_{u_i \in \mathcal{U}} |TopN_i \cap I_i|}{\sum_{u_i \in \mathcal{U}} |TopN_i|}$$
$$recall@N = \frac{\sum_{u_i \in \mathcal{U}} |TopN_i \cap I_i|}{\sum_{u_i \in \mathcal{U}} |I_i|},$$

where $TopN_i$ is the set of N items recommended to user u_i that u_i has not been associated in the training set, and I_i is the set of items that have been associated with u_i in the testing set. A larger precision@N or recall@N value means better performance. The values of precision@N and recall@N are usually small in the case of sparse datasets. For example, the precision@5 is less than 0.05 over a dataset with 8.02e-3 density. Long recommendation lists typically improve recall, while reducing precision. Therefore, F-score is a metric combining them, and it is less dependent on the length of the recommendation list. For example, F1-score is formally defined as:

$$\text{F1-score} = \frac{2 * precision * recall}{precision + recall}.$$

Another popular metric is Discount Cumulative Gain (DCG), which is defined as

$$DCG = \sum_{i=1}^{b} r_i + \sum_{i=b+1}^{L} \frac{r_n}{\log_b i},$$

where r_i indicates the relevance of the i-th ranked item (r_i = 1 for a relevant item and zero otherwise), b a persistence parameter which was usually empirically set to 2, L the ranked list of recommended items. The intention of DCG is that highly ranked relevant items give more satisfaction and utility than badly ranked ones.

Diversity and Novelty

Diversity metrics assess how different the items recommended by a recommend systems. There are two types of diversity metrics, i.e., inter-user diversity and intra-user diversity. Inter-user diversity evaluates the ability of a recommender system to return different results to different users, i.e., the diversity of recommendation lists between users. For example, for u_i and u_j, the inter-user diversity of Top-N recommendations is formally defined as:

$$ED(i, j) = 1 - \frac{Q(i, j)}{N},$$

where $Q(i, j)$ is the number of common items shared by u_i and u_j in their top-n recommendation lists. If their lists are identical, $ED(i, j) = 0$, while if their lists are completely different $ED(i, j) = 1$. The greater the value of ED, the more diverse recommendations the system makes. Assume that $\mathcal{L} = \{v_1, \dots, v_N\}$ is the top-N recommendation list for u_i and the intra-user diversity is defined as:

$$AD(i) = \frac{1}{N(N-1)} \sum_{v_i, v_j \in \mathcal{L} \wedge i \neq j} s(v_i, v_j),$$

where $s(v_i, v_j)$ is the similarity between v_i and v_j, which can be obtained either from the input ratings or from item content. The lower the value of AD, the more diverse recommendations the system makes.

Novelty metrics assess how different the items recommended by a recommender system with respect to what the users have already seen before. One intuitive novelty metric is to measure the average popularity of the recommended items as:

$$Novelty = \frac{1}{n * L} \sum_{i=1}^{n} \sum_{v_j \in L_i} P_j,$$

where L is the length of the recommendation list, L_i the recommendation item list for u_i and P_j the popularity of the item v_j. Lower popularity indicates higher novelty of the recommendations. Another metrics are based on self-information of recommended items such as the discovery-based novelty, which considers the probability that an item is known or familiar to a random user

Coverage

Coverage metrics include item coverage and user coverage. Item coverage measures the percentage of items that a recommender system is able to recommend to users. Let N_c be the total number of unique items in the top-N recommendation lists over all users, i.e., the size of $\cup_{i=1}^{n} L_i$, and then the coverage in a Top-N recommender system is calculated as:

$$Coverage = \frac{N_c}{L}.$$

Low item coverage suggests that the system can access and recommend only a small number of items (usually the most popular ones) which often results in little diverse recommendations. User coverage evaluates the percentage of users that a recommender system can recommend items to. Recommending popular items is likely to obtain high accuracy but low coverage. Therefore, coverage is complementary to accuracy metrics since a good recommender system method should be of both high accuracy and coverage.

4.5   RECENT ADVANCES IN TRUST-AWARE RECOMMENDER SYSTEMS

Trust information greatly advances recommendation and there are many successful cases about trust-aware recommender systems. For example, trust information contains complementary information for the improvement of recommendation performance; users' preferences and tastes can be propagated via trust, which can significantly reduce the size of cold-start users; and trust-aware recommender systems can remarkably improve the coverage of recommendation. These successful applications encourage the development of more advanced approaches to exploit trust information.

4.5.1   GLOBAL TRUST IN RECOMMENDATION

As mentioned in Chapter 3, trust can be viewed from both global and local perspectives. Users are likely to seek suggestions from both their local trusted friends and users with high global reputations. In the physical world, user reputation plays an important role in recommendation and many companies employ people with high reputations to enhance consumers' awareness and understanding of their products. Seno and Lukas found that suggestions from people with high reputations positively affect a consumer's adoption of a brand [121]. Naturally, global trust may be helpful in recommendation. LOCABAL [132] provides an approach to capture global trust for recommendation. It first adopts PageRank to compute the user reputation scores, and it then defines user reputation score w_i as a function f of user reputation ranking r_i:

$$w_i = f(r_i) = \frac{1}{1 + log(r_i)},$$

where the function f limits the value of the reputation score w_i within $[0, 1]$ and ensures that top-ranked users have high reputation scores. Finally, LOCABAL captures global trust by weighting the reliability of user ratings according to their reputation scores as

$$\min \sum_{\langle u_i, v_j \rangle \in \mathcal{O}} w_i (\mathbf{R}_{ij} - \mathbf{U}_i^\top \mathbf{V}_j)^2,$$

where the reliability of ratings from u_i is controlled by her/his reputation score w_i. A larger value of w_i, indicating that the ratings from u_i are more reliable, increases the contributions of ratings from u_i to the learning process.

4.5.2   MULTI-FACETED TRUST IN RECOMMENDATION

Many trust-aware recommender systems treat a user's trust homogeneously. However, trust is multi-faceted and is intrinsically context dependence, i.e., people place trust differently to users in different domains [133]. For example, u_i might trust u_j in "Sports" but not trust u_j in "Electronics" at all. Exploiting multi-faceted trust can potentially benefit recommender systems [133]. A circle-based recommender system is proposed in [155]. It first infers users' trust circles and an example of inferred trust circles is illustrated in Figure 4.3. In the figure, each user is labeled with the categories in which he/she has ratings and Part (a) is the original trust network; Parts (b), (c), and (d) are inferred circles for categories c_1, c_2, and c_3, respectively. After obtained trust circles for users, it performs SocialMF to make recommendations within each circle.

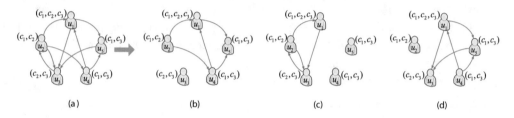

Figure 4.3: An illustration of inferring trust circles. Note that each user is labeled with the categories in which he/she has ratings and (a): the original trust network; (b), (c), and (d) are inferred circles for categories c_1, c_2, and c_3, respectively.

4.5.3   DISTRUST IN RECOMMENDATION

Trust and distrust are shaped by different dimensions of trustworthiness, and trust affects behavioral intentions differently from distrust does. Recent study demonstrates that distrust is not the negation of trust and has significant added value. Distrust tends to be more noticeable and applicable, and weighted more in decision making than trust. There is recent work applying both trust and distrust in recommendation and the research findings demonstrate that distrust can improve the recommendation performance. Distrust is discussed in the Chapter 5.

CHAPTER 5

Incorporating Distrust

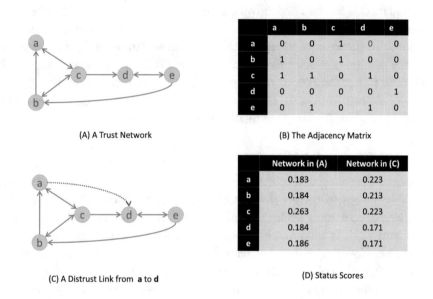

	a	b	c	d	e
a	0	0	1	0	0
b	1	0	1	0	0
c	1	1	0	1	0
d	0	0	0	0	1
e	0	1	0	1	0

(A) A Trust Network

(B) The Adjacency Matrix

	Network in (A)	Network in (C)
a	0.183	0.223
b	0.184	0.213
c	0.263	0.223
d	0.184	0.171
e	0.186	0.171

(C) A Distrust Link from **a** to **d**

(D) Status Scores

Figure 5.1: The importance of distrust in trust computing.

Compared with trust, little attention is paid to distrust in social media. Research with only trust may be biased without considering distrust [44, 138]. As mentioned before, trust relations can be represented as a trust network and the adjacency matrix is adopted to represent the trust network where "0" is often used to indicate no trust. A typical example of a binary trust network is illustrated in Figure 5.1 (A) and (B). However, this representation may not be representative since a zero score cannot distinguish between distrust and no trust. For example, a distrust relation may exist from node *a* to node *d* as shown in Figure 5.1 (C). Furthermore, ignoring distrust in social media applications may lead to over-estimation of the effects of trust [142]. The first column of Table (D) in Figure 5.1 shows reputation scores, calculated using PageRank [110], of nodes in the network of Figure 5.1 (A); while the second column shows reputation scores, calculated by a variant of Pagerank taking into account distrust [142], of nodes in the network of Figure 5.1 (C). The only difference between networks in Figure 5.1 (A) and (C) is a distrust relation from *a* to *d* in the network (C); clearly, the small difference significantly affects the statuses of the nodes. This example illustrates that distrust could be as important as trust and we should not ignore distrust in trust computing. In this chapter, we discuss incorporating distrust into trust computing tasks including representing trust, measuring trust and applying trust.

5.1   INCORPORATING DISTRUST INTO TRUST REPRESENTATIONS

Computational models for trust depend on certain trust representations [139]; hence, an immediate question to incorporate distrust into trust computing is how to incorporate distrust into trust representations. To incorporate distrust into trust representations, a fundamental problem is to understand the relation between trust and distrust since different understandings of distrust over trust could result in representations substantially different. In this section, we first introduce understandings of distrust from social sciences, then a computational understanding and properties of distrust with social media data, and finally their corresponding representations.

5.1.1   UNDERSTANDINGS FROM SOCIAL SCIENCES

In social sciences, the conceptual counterpart of trust, distrust, has been widely investigated. Distrust is probably the only construct that can be even more complex than trust [48]. For example, trust has a dozen of constructs while there are several different interpretations of distrust for each construct of trust [23]. It is commonly believed that trust is a desired property and distrust is an unwanted one. However, certain behavior that is commonly attributed to distrust is not only individually justifiable but also socially desired; hence, distrust has its rightful place among tools that we use within the society. Distrust could be as important as trust [23, 48]. For example, both trust and distrust could help a decision maker reduce uncertainty and vulnerability (i.e., risk) associated with decision consequences [22] and only distrust can irrevocably exclude services from being selected at all [23].

An enduring question about distrust among social scientists is "What is the relation between trust and distrust?" This question has its significance in the task of incorporating distrust. If trust and distrust are the same or equivalent, lack of distrust research matters little; however, if they are different, the lack of distrust research could be problematic because distrust may have unique impact. One understanding of their relation is that distrust is the negation of trust. For example, similar to trust, distrust is considered as a tool to restrict complexity and is a functional equivalent of distrust [86] and distrust is also simply treated as a low level of trust, hence evidence of high trust was always regarded as that of low distrust, and outcomes of high trust would be identical to those of low distrust [61]. An alternative understanding is that distrust is not a simple reversal of the concept of trust [94] and it is a concept separated from trust [80]. For example, three reasons are proposed to prove that trust and distrust are separate: (1) they separate empirically; (2) they coexist; and (3) they have different antecedents and consequents [80, 94, 101]. Some social scientists consider distrust as the "darker" side of trust [94] and there is still no consensus about the answer.

5.1.2   AN COMPUTATIONAL UNDERSTANDING IN SOCIAL MEDIA

Social media data does not contain as much information as social scientists ascribe in their distrust studying, because more often than not, available social media data is from passive observation. Understanding distrust in social media requires new methods since those from social sciences are not directly applicable, but can be helpful in the search of new methods. Given the scale of social media data, it is possible to leverage computational tools such as data mining and machine learning techniques for a computational understanding of distrust in social media. Typically, a computational understanding of distrust seeks answers for the following questions: (1) what are the properties of distrust?; (2) is distrust the negation of trust?; and (2) does distrust have added value over trust?

Properties of Distrust

Properties of trust help determine the value of trust [40]. Hence, to understand distrust, it is natural to start with exploring properties of distrust especially whether there are some obvious connections between these properties of trust to distrust. Studying properties of distrust can help understand how unique distrust is and what the intrinsic differences are between trust and distrust.

Power-law distributions: It is well known that the distributions of incoming or outgoing trust relations for users in a trust network usually follow power-law-like distributions—a few users with large degrees while most users with few degrees. In [138], incoming or outgoing distrust relations for each user in a distrust network are calculated and there are two important findings—(a) trust networks are much denser than distrust networks; and (b) for users with distrust relations, the degree distributions also follow power-law-like distributions—a few users with a large number of distrust relations, while most users with few distrust relations, as shown in Figure 5.2.

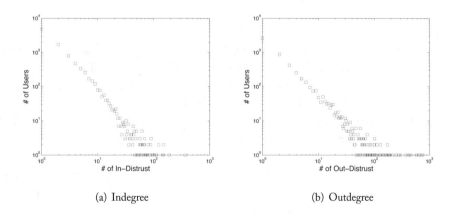

(a) Indegree   (b) Outdegree

Figure 5.2: The distributions of indegree and outdegree of distrust relations.

Low Clustering Coefficient: Trust relations are clusterizable and present high clustering coefficients (CC). Actually, high values of CC are expected because of the cohesive nature of trust relations and the benefits of communities [25]. However, the values of clustering coefficients for distrust relations are significantly lower than these for trust relations, which suggests that certain mechanisms such as triadic closure cannot be applied to distrust relations [126].

Transitivity: It is a primary property of trust and it describes that trust can be propagated between people [40]. For example, if user u_i trusts user u_j, and user u_j trusts user u_k, then transitivity indicates that with a high probability, user u_i trusts user u_k. Tang et al. [138] examined the transitivity of distrust in the Epinions dataset - when u_i distrusts u_j and u_j distrusts u_k, if there is a relation from u_i to u_k, the probability of u_i trusting u_k is much higher than that of u_i distrusting u_j, which suggests that distrust is less likely to be transitive.

Asymmetry: The asymmetry of trust is also important and suggests that for two people involved in a relation, trust is not necessarily identical in both directions [38]. For example, if u_i trusts u_j, one cannot infer that u_j trusts u_i. Distrust is even more asymmetric. For example, Tang et al. [138] observed that there are 37.71% mutual trust relations, but only 5.86% mutual distrust relations in the Epinons dataset.

Correlation with Similarity: Ziegler et al. [168] point out that there is a strong and significant correlation between trust and similarity, and users with trust relations are more similar than those without. However, users are likely to be more similar to users with distrust than those without any links while users with trust are likely to be more similar than those with distrust [138]. These observations suggest that distrust in social media exhibits unique properties and may not be indicator of neither similarity nor dissimilarity.

Is Distrust the Negation of Trust?

Some social scientists believe distrust as the negation of trust-trust and distrust are two ends of the same conceptual spectrum, and distrust can be interpreted by low trust. To answer the question of "is distrust the negation of trust?," a task of predicting distrust from only trust is designed [138]. It reasons as follows: if distrust is the negation of trust, distrust can be suggested for pairs of users with low trust, consequently we can accurately predict distrust from only trust. Hence, the problem of predicting distrust from only trust boils down to the problem of predicting low trust with only trust.

In a trust network, trust scores for pairs without explicit trust relations can be predicted by algorithms in measuring trust introduced in Chapter 3; hence, a general framework for the task is shown in Algorithm 1. The input of the framework includes the trust network $\mathbf{T}$ and an algorithm for measuring trust f. For a pair of users without explicit trust $\langle u_i, u_j \rangle$, f is used to calculate a trust score $\tilde{\mathbf{T}}_{ij}$ from u_i to u_j and then distrust relations are suggested to pairs with low trust scores.

Algorithm 1 A general framework of predicting distrust from only trust

---

Input: User-user trust relation matrix $\mathbf{T}$, and an algorithm of measuring trust f
Output: Ranking list of pairs of users
 1: Extracting pairs $\langle u_i, u_j \rangle$ without explicit trust relations into a set of $\mathcal{Z}$
 2: **for** each pair of users $\langle u_i, u_j \rangle \in \mathcal{Z}$ **do**
 3:    Predicting the trust score of $\tilde{\mathbf{T}}_{ij}$ from u_i to u_j by f
 4: **end for**
 5: Ranking pairs of users (e.g., $\langle u_i, u_j \rangle$) according to $\tilde{\mathbf{T}}_{ij}$ in an ascending order.

Tang et al. evaluated the task of predicting distrust with only trust in the Epinions dataset in Tang. et al. [138]. Two representative algorithms of measuring trust, i.e., trust propagation [44] and matrix factorization-based method [132] are experienced. If distrust is the negation of trust, low trust scores should accurately indicate distrust. However, the performance of using low trust scores to predict distrust is even consistently worse than that of randomly guessing, i.e., low trust scores fail to predict distrust; hence, distrust is not the negation of trust. Social scientists who support distrust not the negation of trust suggest that pairs of users with untrust (or lack of trust) can also have very low trust scores, which is especially applicable for users in social media since they are distributed world wide.

Does Distrust Have Added Value over Trust?
An alternative understanding from social sciences is that distrust is not the negation of trust and it has added value over trust. Therefore, the task of trust prediction with information from distrust is designed to verify if distrust has added value over trust. The intuition behind this task is if distrust has added value over trust, distrust should provide extra information about users and we will be able to predict trust better with distrust information.

Essentially, the task of trust prediction with information from distrust is to incorporate distrust into the task of trust measuring. Recently, researchers attempt to incorporate distrust into algorithms of measuring trust such as trust propagation with distrust [44] and matrix factorization with trust and distrust [132]. Since the task is actually the task of incorporating distrust into task measuring, we ignore details about details and an overview of those algorithms will be presented in the next section. Empirical findings of those algorithms with social media datasets suggest that a small number of distrust relations can significantly improve the performance of trust prediction, indicating that distrust has added value over trust.

5.1.3   DISTRUST IN TRUST REPRESENTATIONS
With the computational understanding of the relations between trust and distrust, we discuss their corresponding representations. If distrust is considered as the negation of trust, high (or low) trust would be identical to those of low (or high) distrust. In this case, we represent trust

and distrust as two ends of the same conceptual spectrum; hence, we do not need to change trust representations and only identify low trust as distrust in the original representations. If distrust is not the negation of trust, there are two views about the relations between trust and distrust.

- Trust and distrust are viewed as tightly related features in a single structure [77]. Hence, we add positive and negative signs to represent trust and distrust respectively, and we keep the semantics of a zero score in the representation; and

- Distrust is viewed as a distinct dimension from trust about users [126]. Hence, we add a new dimension about users to represent distrust.

To better understand the aforementioned three representations, we illustrate these representations from a network perspective as demonstrated in Figure 5.3. Note that we only illustrate incorporating distrust into single-dimensional trust representations since similar illustrations can be applied to multi-dimensional trust representations. When we consider distrust as low trust, the trust and distrust network is a weighted unsigned network, as shown in Figure 5.3(a), when we add signs to represent trust and distrust, the resulting network is a signed network as shown in Figure 5.3(b), while we add a new dimension to represent distrust, the trust and distrust network is a two-dimensional unsigned network as shown, in Figure 5.3(c).

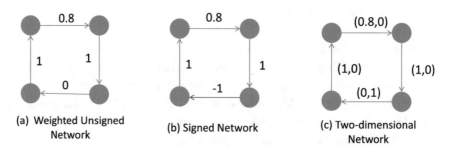

Figure 5.3: Network understandings of representations of trust and distrust.

If we consider trust and distrust relations as tightly related features in a single network. We represent both trust and distrust relations into one adjacency matrix $\mathbf{F} \in \mathbb{R}^{n \times n}$ where $\mathbf{F}_{ij} \in (0, 1]$, $\mathbf{F}_{ij} \in [-1, 0)$ and $\mathbf{F}_{ij} = 0$ denote trust, distrust, and missing relations from u_i to u_j, respectively. If we tread distrust as a distinct dimension from trust about users, we use two adjacency matrices to represent trust and distrust links, separately. In particular, we use $\mathbf{T} \in \mathbb{R}^{n \times n}$ to represent trust relations where $\mathbf{T}_{ij} \in (0, 1]$ and $\mathbf{T}_{ij} = 0$ denote a trust relation and a missing relation from u_i to u_j. Similarly, $\mathbf{D} \in \mathbb{R}^{n \times n}$ is used to represent distrust relations where $\mathbf{D}_{ij} \in (0, 1]$ and $\mathbf{D}_{ij} = 0$ denote a distrust relation and a missing relation from u_i to u_j. It is easy to convert one representation into the other representation with the following rules: $\mathbf{F} = \mathbf{T} - \mathbf{D}$, and $\mathbf{T} = \frac{|\mathbf{F}| + \mathbf{F}}{2}$ and $\mathbf{D} = \frac{|\mathbf{F}| - \mathbf{F}}{2}$ where $|\mathbf{F}|$ is the absolution of $\mathbf{F}$.

5.1.4 SOCIAL THEORIES FOR TRUST/DISTRUST NETWORKS

When we add positive and negative signs to represent trust and distrust, the resulting trust/distrust networks become a special type of signed networks where trust and distrust relations are positive and negative relations, respectively. Two social theories, i.e., balance theory [50] and status theory [44, 78], have been proven to be very helpful in mining signed social networks [78], which are also very important in incorporating distrust into computational tasks of trust [130].

Balance Theory

Balance theory is originated in Heider [50] at the individual level and generalized by Cartwright and Harary [15] in the graph-theoretical formation at the group level. When the signed network is not restricted to be complete, the network is balanced if all its cycles have an even number of negative links. Using that definition, it is proven in Harary et al. [47] that "a signed graph is balanced if and only if nodes can be separated into two mutually exclusive subsets such that each positive link joins two nodes of the same subset and each negative link joins nodes from different subsets." It is difficult to represent real-world signed networks by balanced structure therefore Davis [27] introduced the notion of clusterizable graph—a signed graph is clusterizable if there exists a partition of the nodes such that nodes with positive links are in the same subset and nodes with negative links are between different subsets.

Social balance researchers have proposed some important metrics to measure the degree of balance of given signed networks, which are based on the number of balanced or unbalanced cycles. One way is to calculate the ratio of balanced circles among all possible circles by using the adjacency matrix [14], which was modified to consider the length of cycles in Henley et al. [51]. The time complexity of these metrics is normally $O(n^3)$, which is infeasible for large real-world signed networks and Terzi and Winkler, proposed a computational algorithm to evaluate the degree of balance in Terzi and Winkler [141].

Balance theory generally implies that "the friend of my friend is my friend" and "the enemy of my enemy is my friend" [50]. For signed networks in social media, we often consider the balance of triangles. Basically, it considers the balance of signs on a triad involving three nodes in signed networks. Let s_{ij} represent the sign of the link between from u_i to u_j where $s_{ij} = 1$ and $s_{ij} = -1$ denote a positive link and a negative link are observed between u_i and u_j. Balance theory suggests that a triad $\langle u_i, u_j, u_k \rangle$ is balanced if - (1) $s_{ij} = 1$ and $s_{jk} = 1$, then $s_{ik} = 1$; or (2) $s_{ij} = -1$ and $s_{jk} = -1$, then $s_{ik} = 1$.

For a triad, four possible sign combinations exist, as demonstrated in Figure 5.4. Among these four combinations - **A**(+,+,+), **B**(+,+,-) **C**(+,-,-), and **D**(-,-,-), **A** and **C** are balanced. The way to measure the balance of signed networks in social media is to examine all these triads and then to compute the ratio of **A** and **C** over **A**, **B**, **C**, and **D**. Existing work reported that triads in signed networks in social media are highly balanced. For example, Leskovec et al. [77] found that ratios of balanced triads of signed networks in Epinions, Slashdot, and Wikipedia are 0.941, 0.912, and 0.909, respectively; and more than 90% of triads are balanced in other social media datasets [154]. Furthermore, the ratio of balanced triads increases while unbalanced triads decreases over time [126].

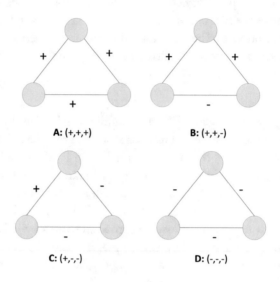

Figure 5.4: An illustration of balance theory. **A** and **C** are balanced, and **B** and **D** are imbalanced.

Status Theory

While balance theory is developed for undirected signed networks, for directed signed networks, status theory is introduced in Guha et al. [44] and Leskovec et al. [78]. Social status indicates rankings of nodes in social networks, and represents the degree of honor or prestige of nodes. In general, status theory suggests that u_i has a higher status than u_j if there is a positive link from u_j to u_i or a negative link from u_i to u_j.

In directed social networks, there are two types of triads as shown in Figure 5.5—(1) acyclic triads T_1 and (2) cyclic triads T_2. For cyclic triads, there are four possible sign combinations, hence there are four types of cyclic signed triads for T_2, as shown in Figure 5.6. Each link in an acyclic triad can be positive or negative and signs of links in a acyclic triad are not exchangeable; hence there are eight types of acyclic signed triads, as depicted in Figure 5.7. Overall, there are 12 types of possible triads in directed signed networks.

A popular procedure to examine whether a given triad satisfies status theory or not is: reversing directions of all negative links, flipping their signs to positive, if the resulting triad is acyclic, then the triad satisfies status theory. Following the procedure, we find that 8 of 12 types of triads in signed networks satisfy status theory as shown in the first row of Table 5.1. Similar to the way to measure the balance of signed networks, we examine all 12 triads and then to calculate the

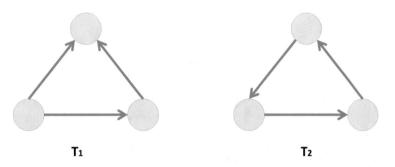

Figure 5.5: Possible triads in directed social networks.

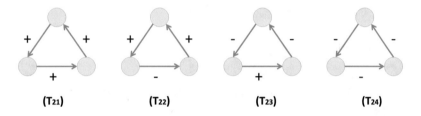

Figure 5.6: An illustration of four types of cyclic signed triads.

Table 5.1: Balance theory vs. status theory. Note that "✓" means "satisfy" the corresponding theory

	T_{11}	T_{12}	T_{13}	T_{14}	T_{15}	T_{16}	T_{17}	T_{18}	T_{21}	T_{22}	T_{23}	T_{24}
Status Theory	✓	✓		✓	✓	✓		✓		✓	✓	
Balance Theory	✓				✓	✓	✓		✓		✓	

ratio of triads satisfying status theory. Examinations on signed networks in social media suggest that more than 90% of triads satisfy status theory [78].

Status theory and balance theory do not always agree with each other as shown in Table 5.1 where "✓" means "satisfy" the corresponding theory. Some triads satisfy both theories such as the triad T_{11}; some satisfy status theory but contradict with balance theory such as the triad T_{12}; some satisfy balance theory but contradict with status theory such as the triad T_{21}; while others contradict with both such as the triad T_{24}.

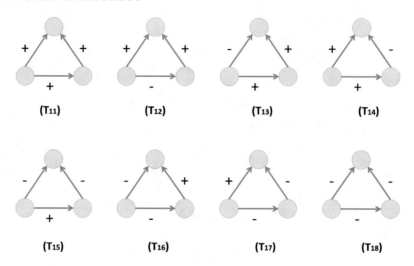

Figure 5.7: An illustration of eight types of acyclic signed triads.

5.2   INCORPORATING DISTRUST INTO PREDICTING TRUST

An increasing number of researchers accept that distrust has added value, which results in a large body of literature about incorporating distrust into trust metrics. The purpose of incorporating distrust into trust metrics is two-fold. First, it can make use of the added value of distrust to refine trust metrics. Second, it may infer new trust and distrust simultaneously especially for local trust metrics. A classification of existing algorithms of measuring trust has been introduced in Chapter 3 and following the same classification, next we will first review algorithms of distrust in global trust metrics, and then algorithms of distrust in local trust metrics including supervised and unsupervised methods.

5.2.1   DISTRUST IN GLOBAL TRUST METRICS

Incorporating distrust into global trust metrics is to calculate global trustworthy scores of users in a network by considering both trust and distrust relations, which focuses on how to incorporate distrust to improve global trust metrics. Since distrust relations are usually not considered, most global trust metrics cannot deal with distrust directly [24, 49]. As shown in Figure 5.1, distrust may have big impact on the trustworthy scores of users in a trust network and many algorithms are proposed to obtain more accurate trustworthy scores for users by incorporating distrust.

If a node receives many incoming trust, it should have high prestige value, while nodes with many incoming distrust should decrease their values of prestige. A metric based on the indegree of trust and distrust relations is proposed in [170] as:

$$p_i = \frac{|I_i^+| - |I_i^-|}{|I_i^+| + |I_i^-|},$$

where $|I_i^+|$, $|I_i^-|$, and p_i are the indegree of trust relations, the indegree of distrust relations, and the trustworthy score of u_i, respectively. A similar metric is used in Kunegis et al. [74] as the subtraction of indegree of distrust relations from indegree of trust relations, i.e., $p_i = |I_i^+| - |I_i^-|$.

PageRank is one of the most popular global trust metrics and several efforts are conducted to incorporate distrust into PageRank. In [122], two scores are calculated by the original PageRank algorithm for the trust network and the distrust network separately, and the final scores are the subtractions of scores for the trust network from those for the distrust network. This algorithm considers trust and distrust separately and completely ignores the interactions between them. We can also attempt the following assumption that should trust nodes with negative reputation scores less instead of distrusting them. With this assumption, an algorithm based on discrete choice theory is proposed in Traag et al. [142]. If the observed reputation is $k_i = \sum_{u_j \in I_i} \mathbf{F}_{ji} p_j$, the probability of u_i with the highest real reputation according to discrete choice theory is:

$$p_i = \frac{exp(k_i/\mu)}{\sum_j exp(k_j/\mu)},$$

then we obtain a recursive formulation for the algorithm to compute trustworthy scores as:

$$\mathbf{p}^{t+1} = \frac{exp(1/\mu \mathbf{F}^\top \mathbf{p}^t)}{\|exp(1/\mu \mathbf{F}^\top \mathbf{p}^t)\|_1}.$$

Within a certain range of μ, the above iterative formulation can achieve a global solution $\mathbf{p}^*$ with arbitrary initial conditions.

In the process of random walk, walkers may try to avoid walking via distrust. Therefore, users receiving distrust relations are visited less as compared to those with trust relations. With this intuition, a new formulation based on the original PageRank algorithm [29] is proposed to handle distrust as:

$$\mathbf{p}_i^{t+1} = (1 - \hat{\mathbf{Q}}_{ii}^t)(\alpha \sum_{u_j \in I_i^+} \frac{\mathbf{p}_j^t}{O_j^+} + (1 - \alpha)\frac{1}{N}),$$

where $\hat{\mathbf{Q}}_{ii}^t$ denotes the percentage of walkers that distrust the user they are in. In that manner, $(1 - \hat{\mathbf{Q}}_{ii}^t)$ represents the percentage of remaining walkers in u_i. The distrust matrix $\hat{\mathbf{Q}}$ is calculated as follows:

- A walker moves as a random walker in the original PageRank algorithm and keeps his opinion as

$$\hat{\mathbf{Q}}^{t+1} = \mathbf{Z}^t \mathbf{Q}^t,$$

where $\mathbf{Z}$ is the transition matrix with $\mathbf{Z}_{ij}^t$ indicating the percentage of walkers from u_i who were in u_j at time t.

- A walker in u_i automatically adopts negative opinions of u_i, that is, he adds the users distrusted by u_i into his distrust list. $(\mathbf{Q}_{ij}^{t+1} = -1)$ and a walker who distrusts a user leaves the graph if ever he visits the node $(\mathbf{Q}_{ij}^{t+1} = 0)$:

$$\mathbf{Q}_{ij}^{t+1} = \begin{cases} 1 & \text{if } \mathbf{F}_{ij} = -1 , \\ 0 & \text{if } i = j , \\ \hat{\mathbf{Q}}_{ij}^{t+1} & \text{otherwise} \end{cases},$$

The concepts of bias and deserve are introduced in Mishra and Bhattacharya [103] to handle distrust where bias (or trustworthiness) of a link reflects the expected weight of an outgoing connection and deserve (or prestige) of a link reflects the expected weight of an incoming connection from an unbiased user. The deserve score DES_i for u_i is the aggregation of all unbiased votes from her incoming connections as:

$$DES_i^{t+1} = \frac{1}{|I_i|} \sum_j \mathbf{F}_{ji}(1 - X_{ji}^t),$$

where X_{ji} indicates the influence that bias of u_j has on its outgoing link to u_i

$$X_{ji} = \max\{0, BIAS_j * \mathbf{F}_{ji}\},$$

while the bias score $BIAS_i$ for u_i is the aggregation of voting biases of her outgoing connections as:

$$BIAS_i^{t+1} = \frac{1}{2 * |O_i|} \sum_{u_j \in O_i} (A_{ji} - DES_j^t),$$

5.2.2   DISTRUST IN LOCAL TRUST METRICS

Incorporating distrust into local trust metrics, also known as the problem of trust and distrust prediction, is to infer new trust and distrust relations by leveraging old trust and distrust relations. Existing algorithms can be generally grouped into supervised methods and unsupervised methods.

Unsupervised Methods

Unsupervised methods are usually based on certain topological properties of given trust/distrust networks. According to the adopted topological properties, algorithms in this family can be further divided into similarity-based, propagation-based, and low-rank approximation-based methods. Note that the vast majority of existing unsupervised algorithms represent trust and distrust by adding signs (or they consider trust an distrust networks as signed networks).

Similarity-based Methods   Similarity-based methods predict trust and distrust relations based on user similarity. A typical similarity-based method consists of two steps. It first defines a similarity metric to calculate user similarities and then it provides a component to predict trust and distrust relations (or signs) based on those user similarities.

There are two popular ways to calculate user similarities: (a) clustering-based methods and (b) status theory-based methods. Clustering-based methods calculate user similarities based on user clustering in trust/distrust networks. Below are two representative approaches to compute user similarity based on user clusters.

- It first clusters the network into a number of clusters using the user clustering algorithm in Doreian and Mrvar [31], and then the conditional similarity for two clusters A and B with a third cluster C is defined as [60]:

$$Sim_{A,B|C} = \frac{\sum_{s \in S_{A,B|C}} m_{A,s} m_{B,s}}{\sqrt{s \in S_{A,B|C} m_{A,s}^2} \sqrt{s \in S_{A,B|C} m_{B,s}^2}},$$

  where $S_{A,B|C}$ is the set of users in the cluster C, which are linked by users in A and B, and $m_{A,s}$ the average signs of links from users in cluster A to node s. User similarity is calculated as the similarity between clusters where these two users are assigned.

- Spectral clustering based on Laplacian matrix [54] for trust/distrust networks is performed first [124] and then define two similarities:

  (1) the similarity of users that are assigned to the same cluster:

$$simSC(i, j) = 1 - \|D(i, c_i) - D(j, c_j)\|;$$

  (2) the similarity of users that are assigned to different clusters

$$simDC(i, j) = \frac{1}{1 + D(i, c_i) + D(j, c_j)},$$

  where $D(.,.)$ is a distance metric, and c_i is the i-th cluster of users.

Status theory-based methods calculate user similarities based on status theory. According to status theory, the users' in-degree of trust $|I^+|$ and the users' out-degree $|O^-|$ of distrust increase their statuses. In contrast, the users' out-degree of trust $|O^-|$, and the users' in-degree $|I^-|$ of distrust decrease their statuses. With above intuitions, a similarity metric based on status theory is defined as [125]:

$$sim(i, j) = \frac{1}{\sigma(i) + \sigma(j) - 1}$$
$$\sigma(i) = |I_i^+| + |O_i^-| - |O_i^+| - |I_i^-|.$$

With user similarities, similarity-based methods then determine the signs of links and below are two representative approaches to determine the signs based on user similarities.

- Since we have pair-wise user similarities, collaborative filtering techniques especially user-oriented collaborative filtering can be used to aggregate signs from ones' similar nodes to predict trust and distrust relations [60].

- Based on status theory, the sign from u_i to u_j can be predicted as $sign(sim(i, k) + sim(k, j))$ [125].

Propagation-based Methods   In Guha et al. [44], trust propagation is treated as a repeating sequence of matrix operations, which consists of four types of atomic trust propagations: direct propagation, trust coupling, co-citation, and transpose trust. Two strategies are studied to incorporate distrust.

- One-step distrust propagation: first propagating multiple-step trust and then propagating one-step distrust. The formulation of one-step distrust propagation with k-step trust propagation is:

$$\tilde{\mathbf{T}} = \sum_{k=1}^{K} \gamma^k \mathbf{C}^k (\mathbf{T} - \mathbf{D}),$$

where $\mathbf{C}^k$ is the result after k-step trust propagation and you can find more details about $\mathbf{C}^k$ in Chapter 3.

- Multiple-step distrust propagation: propagating trust and distrust propagate together. Instead of propagating only trust with four types of atomic trust propagations, this strategy propagates both trust and distrust. The formulation of propagating both trust and distrust is presented below:

$$\mathbf{E} = \alpha_1 \mathbf{F} + \alpha_2 \mathbf{F}^\top \mathbf{F} + \alpha_3 \mathbf{F}^\top + \alpha_4 \mathbf{F} \mathbf{F}^\top.$$

After k-step propagation, similar to trust propagation, the final results of trust/distrust propagation is an aggregation of the result of each step as:

$$\hat{\mathbf{F}} = \sum_{k=1}^{K} \gamma^k \mathbf{E}^k.$$

Empirical findings indicate that one-step distrust propagation often outperforms multiple-step distrust propagation [44]. However, one-step distrust propagation might not converge in trust/distrust networks dominated by distrust, while multiple-step distrust propagation may yield some unexpected behaviors [169]. To mitigate those two problems, Ziegler and Lausen [169] proposed integrating distrust into the process of the Appleseed trust metric computation instead of superimposing distrust afterwards. Methods in Guha et al. [44] and Ziegler and Lausen [169] are based on the matrix operations. There are methods in this family investigating other operations such as subjective logic [68], intuitionistic fuzzy relations [28], and bilattice [144], which can naturally perform both trust and distrust propagation.

Low-Rank Approximation Methods   The notion of balance is generalized by Davis [27] to weak balance. Weak balance theory allows triads with all distrust relations. Therefore in addition to triads $\mathbf{A}$ and $\mathbf{C}$ in Figure 5.4, the triad $\mathbf{D}$ is also weakly balanced. Low-rank approximation methods are based on weak structural balance as suggested in Hsieh et al. [55] that weakly balanced networks have a low-rank structure and weak structural balance in trust/distrust networks naturally suggests low-rank models for trust/distrust networks. In Hsieh et al. [55], the trust/distrust prediction problem is mathematically modeled as a low-rank matrix factorization problem:

$$\min_{\mathbf{U},\mathbf{W}} \quad \|\mathbf{F} - \mathbf{U}\mathbf{W}^{\top}\|_F^2 + \alpha\|\mathbf{U}\|_F^2 + \beta\|\mathbf{W}\|_F^2.$$

The square function is chosen as the loss function in Hsieh et al. [55]. Pair-wise empirical error, similar to the hinge loss convex surrogate for 0/1 loss in classification, is used in Agrawal et al. [3]. They use this particular variation since it elegantly captures the correlations amongst the users and thereby makes the technique more robust to fluctuations in individual behaviors. In Cen et al. [18], a low-rank tensor model is proposed for dynamic trust and distrust prediction problem. Trust/distrust networks are special cases of signed networks, therefore social theories such as balance theory and status theory can be exploited to help trust/distrust prediction. A one-dimensional latent factor r_i is introduced for u_i and then the sign between u_i and u_j is modeled as $r_i r_j$ to capture balance theory. A trust/distrust framework based on matrix factorization is proposed in Tang et al. [135] as:

$$\min_{\mathbf{U},\mathbf{V}} \quad \|\mathbf{F} - \mathbf{U}\mathbf{V}^{\top} - \lambda\mathbf{r}\mathbf{r}^{\top}\|_F^2 + \alpha\|\mathbf{U}\|_F^2 + \beta\|\mathbf{W}\|_F^2 + \lambda\|\mathbf{r}\|_2^2,$$

where $\mathbf{r} = [r_1, r_2, \ldots, r_n]$ and the term $\lambda\mathbf{r}\mathbf{r}^{\top}$ is to capture balance theory in the problem of trust/distrust prediction.

Supervised Methods
Supervised methods consider trust/distrust prediction as classification problems [139]. Supervised methods have several advantages over unsupervised methods such as superior performance, adaptability to different data domains, and variance reduction [83]. It usually consists of two important steps. One is to prepare labeled data and the other is to construct features for each pair of users. The first step can be trivial since trust and distrust relations can be naturally treated as labels. Therefore, algorithms in this family provide different approaches to construct features.

In addition to indegrees and outdegrees of trust (or distrust) relations, triangle-based features according to balance theory are extracted in Leskovec et al. [77]. Since trust/distrust relations are usually very sparse and most users have few indegrees or outdegrees, many users could have no triangle-based features; besides triangle-based features may not be robust [21]. A trust/distrust prediction algorithm can be developed based on any quantitative social imbalance measure of a trust/distrust network. Hence, k-cycle-based features are proposed in Chiang et al. [21] where triangle-based features are special cases of k-cycle-based features when $k = 3$. In addition to k-cycle-based features, incoming local bias (or the percentage of distrust it receives in all the incoming relations) and outgoing local bias (or the percentage of distrust it gives to all of its outgoing relations) are also reported to be helpful for the performance improvement in trust/distrust prediction [165]. In chemical and biological sciences, the quantitative structure-activity relationship hypothesis suggests that "similar molecules" show "similar activities," e.g., the toxicity of a molecule can be predicted by the alignment of its atoms in the three-dimensional space. Therefore, the structure and network patterns of the ego-networks are strongly associated with the types of their generated links. With this intuition, frequent sub-networks from the ego-networks are used as features in Papaoikonomou et al. [111]. Except for features from topological information, attributes of users such as gender, career interest, hometown, movies are also used as features in Patidar et al. [112] where it first trains a classifier based on these features, then suggests new links and finally refines them which either maintain or enhance the balance index according to balance theory. Other types of features are also used for trust/distrust prediction including user interaction features [32] and review-based features [10]. Interaction features are reported to be more effective than users attribute features in DuBois et al. [32].

5.3   INCORPORATING DISTRUST INTO TRUST-AWARE RECOMMENDER SYSTEMS

In the physical world, we seek recommendations from our trusted friends, which suggests that trust information has potentials to improve recommendation performance. Recommendation becomes one of the most important and popular applications of trust. A comprehensive overview about applying trust in recommendation (or trust-aware recommender systems) is given in Chapter 4. Researchers have noted that distrust may be more noticeable, perceived more credible, and weighted more on a behavioral decision than trust with a similar magnitude [22]. Distrust may be as important as trust for recommendation. In addition to observed ratings, a recommender system with trust and distrust also leverages trust and distrust information. In recent years, incorporating distrust into trust-aware recommender systems has attracted increasing attention. Following the same classification of trust-aware recommender systems, we group those recommender systems into memory-based and model-based systems.

5.3.1   MEMORY-BASED METHODS

Memory-based recommender systems with trust/distrust networks intuitively choose memory-based trust-aware recommender systems especially trust-aware user-oriented models as their basic models [19, 107, 145, 147]. For a typical trust-aware user-oriented model, it first calculates user similarities based on some similarity metrics such as Pearson's correlation coefficient and cosine similarity for pairs with trust as introduced in Chapter 4, and then a missing rating from the i-th user u_i to the j-th item p_j is predicted by aggregating ratings from u_i's trusted users to p_j as:

$$\hat{\mathbf{R}}_{ij} = \hat{r}_i + \frac{\sum_{v \in N_i} W_{iv}(\mathbf{R}_{vj} - \hat{r}_v)}{\sum_{v \in N_i} W_{iv}},$$

where N_i is the set of trusted users of u_i, $\hat{r}_i$ the average rating from u_i, and W_{iv} is the connection strength between u_i and u_v.

There are several general strategies to incorporate distrust into the above user-oriented model.

- We might be more prone to accept recommendations from persons we lack trust, probably because of lack of prior experiences, than from persons we explicitly distrust, resulting from past bad experiences or deceit. Therefore, one way to incorporate distrust is to avoid recommendations from those "unwanted" users [145] as:

$$\hat{\mathbf{R}}_{ij} = \hat{r}_i + \frac{\sum_{v \in N_i \setminus D_i} W_{iv}(\mathbf{R}_{vj} - \hat{r}_v)}{\sum_{v \in N+} W_{iv}},$$

  where D_i is the set of users u_i distrusts.

- It is well known that there is a strong correlation between trust and similarity, and trust provides similarity evidence for recommendation. Therefore, another strategy to incorporate distrust is to consider distrust as negative weights, i.e., considering distrust as dissimilarity measurements [147]:

$$\hat{\mathbf{R}}_{ij} = \hat{r}_i + \frac{\sum_{v \in N_i} W_{iv}(\mathbf{R}_{vj} - \hat{r}_v)}{\sum_{v \in N_i} W_{iv}} - \frac{\sum_{v \in D_i} d_{iv}(\mathbf{R}_{vj} - \hat{r}_v)}{\sum_{v \in D_i} d_{iv}},$$

  where d_{iv} is the dissimilarity between u_i and u_v.

- In reality, trust and distrust relations in trust/distrust networks are very sparse therefore Nalluri [107] proposed a recommender system that first propagates trust and distrust values in trust/distrust networks and then reduces the influence from negative values as:

$$\hat{\mathbf{R}}_{ij} = \hat{r}_i + \frac{\sum_{v \in N_i} (\hat{W}_{iv} - \hat{d}_{iv})(\mathbf{R}_{vj} - \hat{r}_v)}{\sum_{v \in N_i} (\hat{W}_{iv} - \hat{d}_{iv})},$$

  where $\hat{W}_{iv}$ and $\hat{d}_{iv}$ are propagated trust and distrust strengths from u_i to u_v, respectively.

5.3.2 MODEL-BASED METHODS

Model-based recommender systems with distrust use model-based trust-aware recommender systems especially matrix factorization based models as their basic models [35, 88, 128]. Assume that

$\mathbf{U}_i$ is the k-dimensional preference latent factor of u_i and $\mathbf{V}_j$ is the k-dimensional characteristic latent factor of item j p_j. A typical matrix factorization-based collaborative filtering method models the rating from u_i to the j-th item $\mathbf{R}_{ij}$ as the interaction between their latent factors, i.e., $\mathbf{R}_{ij} = \mathbf{U}_i^\top \mathbf{V}_j$. If u_i trusts u_j, u_i and u_j are likely to share similar preferences. Therefore, a state-of-the-art trust-aware recommender system proposed in Ma et al. [91] adds the following term on the matrix-factorization method to minimize the distance of the preference vectors of two users with a trust relation:

$$\min \sum_i \sum_{v \in N_i} W_{iv} \|\mathbf{U}_i - \mathbf{U}_v\|_2^2.$$

If u_i distrusts u_j, it is very likely that u_i thinks that u_j has different tastes from him. With this intuition, for a distrust relation from u_i to u_j, Ma et al. [88] proposed to maximize the distance of their latent factors based on the matrix factorization model as:

$$\max \sum_i \sum_{v \in D_i} d_{iv} \|\mathbf{U}_i - \mathbf{U}_v\|_2^2. \tag{5.1}$$

The underlying assumption of Eq. (5.1) is to consider distrust relations as dissimilarity measurements. However, recent research suggests that distrust may not denote dissimilarity and users with distrust tend to be more similar than randomly selected pairs [128]. It also observes that users with trust relations are likely to be more similar than pairs of users with distrust relations, which is consistent with the extension of the notion of structural balance in [26]—a structure in a trust/distrust network should ensure that users are able to have their "friends" closer than their "foes," i.e., users should sit closer to their "friends" (or users with trust relations) than their "foes" (or users with distrust relations). With this intuition, for $\langle i, j, k \rangle$ where u_i has a trust relation to u_j while has a distrust relation to u_k, the latent factor of u_i should be more similar to the latent factor of u_j than that of u_k to capture trust and distrust relations. In particular, for each triple as $\langle i, j, k \rangle$, a regularization term is added as:

$$\ell(d(\mathbf{U}_i, \mathbf{U}_j), d(\mathbf{U}_i, \mathbf{U}_k)), \tag{5.2}$$

where d is a distance metric and ℓ is a penalty function that assesses the violation of latent factors of users with trust and distrust relations [35]. Possible choices of $\ell(z)$ are the hinge loss function $\ell(z) = \max(0, 1 - z)$ and the logistic loss function $\ell(z) = \log(1 + e^{-z})$.

Since the number of triples as $\langle i, j, k \rangle$ could be very large, the introduced regularization terms in Eq. (5.2) can significantly increase the computational complexity, which makes the recommender system not scalable to large data. Each user u_i has a friend circle $\mathcal{P}_i$ including trusted users by u_i and a foe circle $\mathcal{N}_i$ containing distrusted users by u_i. It is observed that users are likely to be more similar with their "friend" circles than their "foe" circles. A recommender system with trust and distrust RecSSN [128] is proposed based on users' friend and foe circles under the matrix factorization framework. Based on $\mathcal{P}_i$ and $\mathcal{N}_i$, it divide users into three groups below:

- $\mathcal{OP}$ includes users who have only trust relations as $\mathcal{OP} = \{u_i | \mathcal{P}_i \neq \emptyset \cap \mathcal{N}_i = \emptyset\}$;

- $\mathcal{ON}$ includes users who have only distrust relations as $\mathcal{ON} = \{u_i | \mathcal{P}_i = \emptyset \cap \mathcal{N}_i \neq \emptyset\}$; and

- $\mathcal{PN}$ contains users who have both trust and distrust relation as $\mathcal{PN} = \{u_i | \mathcal{P}_i \neq \emptyset \cup \mathcal{N}_i \neq \emptyset\}$.

Then it defines $\bar{U}_i^p$ and $\bar{U}_i^n$ as the average user preferences of u_i's friend circle and foe circle, respectively, as follows:

$$\bar{\mathbf{U}}_i^p = \frac{\sum_{u_j \in \mathcal{P}_i} W_{ij} \mathbf{U}_j}{\sum_{u_j \in \mathcal{P}_i} W_{ij}}, \quad \bar{\mathbf{U}}_i^n = \frac{\sum_{u_j \in \mathcal{N}_i} W_{ij} \mathbf{U}_j}{\sum_{u_j \in \mathcal{N}_i} W_{ij}}.$$

It captures trust/distrust information for those groups separately.

- For a user u_i with only friend circle (or $u_i \in \mathcal{OP}$), following a traditional trust-aware recommender system, it forces u_i's preference close to $\mathcal{P}_i$ by minimizing the following term:

$$\min \quad \|\mathbf{U}_i - \bar{\mathbf{U}}_i^p\|_2^2.$$

- For a user u_i with only his foe circle (or $u_i \in \mathcal{ON}$), this user is likely to be untrustworthy and we should not include in recommendation [145]. Therefore, it ignores information from these users with only foe circles.

- For a user u_i with both friend and foe circles, it forces u_i's preference closer to $\mathcal{P}_i$ than $\mathcal{N}_i$ as:

$$\min \quad \max(0, \|\mathbf{U}_i - \bar{\mathbf{U}}_i^p\|_2^2 - \|\mathbf{U}_i - \bar{\mathbf{U}}_i^n\|_2^2).$$

The number of regularization terms introduced by RecSSN [128] is $n - |ON|$ where $|ON|$ is the number of users with only distrust relations, and it is much smaller than the number of regularization terms in Forsati et al. [35].

5.4   RECENT ADVANCES IN INCORPORATING DISTRUST

Incorporating distrust is still in its early stages of development and an active area of exploration. When we add signs to represent trust and distrust, an unsigned trust network is converted into a signed trust/distrust network. In addition to incorporating distrust into computational tasks of trust, it also cultivates tasks specific to trust/distrust networks such as sign prediction and distrust prediction. The differences among trust/distrust prediction [44], sign prediction [154], and distrust prediction [129, 135] are shown in Figure 5.8:

- As shown in Figure 5.8(a), the trust/distrust prediction predicts new trust and distrust relations from existing trust and distrust relations. The distrust prediction problem, as illustrated in Figure 5.8(b), assumes that distrust is not accessible in data.

- The sign prediction problem as shown in Figure 5.8(c) predicts signs of *already existing* relations. The distrust prediction problem needs to identify the pairs of nodes between which distrust relations *are predicted to* exist.

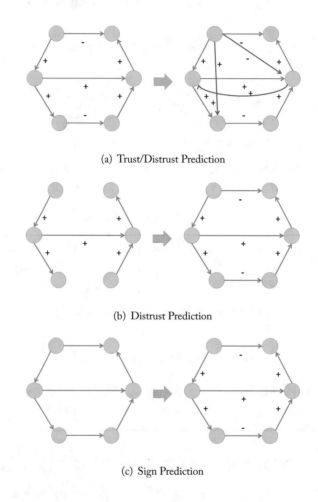

(a) Trust/Distrust Prediction

(b) Distrust Prediction

(c) Sign Prediction

Figure 5.8: An illustration of the differences of trust/distrust prediction, distrust prediction, and sign prediction.

5.4.1 SIGN PREDICTION

The task of sign prediction is to infer the signs of existing unsigned links (or whether an existing link is trust or distrust). It is difficult, if possible, to predict signs of existing links by only utilizing the given unsigned links [135, 138, 154]. Therefore, most of existing sign predictors use additional sources. In reality, we are likely to adopt the opinions from our trusted users while fight against our distrusted users' opinions. As a consequence, decisions of users with trust relations are more likely to agree, whereas for users with distrust relations the chance of disagreement is considerably higher. In social media, users can have positive or negative interactions with other users. Positive interactions show agreement and support, while negative interactions show disagreement and antagonism. There are strong correlations between trust (or distrust) and positive (or negative) interactions [135]. It is evident from these observations that user interaction information should be useful in the problem of sign prediction. Tang et al. suggested a straightforward algorithm for sign prediction based on the correlation between interactions and links: (1) initializing signs of links based on interactions, i.e., positive signs for positive interactions while negative signs for negative interactions; and (2) refining signs of links according to status theory or balance theory [129]. More sophisticated algorithms model link and interaction information into coherent frameworks. In Yang et al. [154], a framework with a set of latent factor models is proposed to infer signs for unsigned links, which captures users' interaction behavior, social relations as well as their interplay. It also models the principles of balance and status theories for trust/distrust networks. A one-dimensional latent factor β_i is introduced for u_i and then the sign between u_i and u_j is modeled as $s_{ij} = \beta_i\beta_j$, which can capture balance theory. The vector parameter η is introduced for users to capture their partial ordering, and then the status ℓ_i of u_i is modeled as $\ell_i = \eta\gamma_i$. Status theory characterizes the sign from u_i to u_j as their relative status difference $\ell_{ij} = \ell_i - \ell_j$. Yu and Xie [159, 160] found that there are high correlation and mutual influence between user interactions and signs of links, and propose a mutual latent random graph framework to flexibly model evidence from user interactions and signs that performs user interaction prediction and sign prediction simultaneously.

5.4.2   DISTRUST PREDICTION

It is suggested in research [48] that trust is a desired property while distrust is often an unwanted one for an online social community. Intuitively, various online services such as Ciao, eBay, and Epinions implement trust mechanisms to help users to better use their services, but few of them allow online users to specify distrust relations. To make use of distrust information, we need to make them visible on social media sites where distrust does not explicitly present. Therefore, it is natural to question whether one can predict distrust information automatically from the available data in social networks. While this problem is very challenging [20], the results of such an approach have the potential to improve the quality of the results of a vast array of applications. Recent works in Tang et al. [129, 135] find that we can reasonably predict distrust by leveraging interaction data and trust relations. There is a strong correlation between negative interactions and distrust relations; hence the concept of pseudo distrust relations is introduced [135]. With pseudo distrust and trust relations, distrust prediction problem is converted into a special trust and distrust prediction problem. Since we are given all trust relations, distrust prediction is to distinguish pairs with distrust relations from the mixture of pairs with distrust and no relations. Distrust prediction can be formulated into a binary classification problem [129].

CHAPTER 6

Epilogue

Every user in social media is allowed to publish, share, and distribute content at any place at any time. On one hand, it generates massive data at an unprecedented rate, resulting in the *information overload* problem that could overwhelm social media users and negatively impact their user experience. With so much information, how can we find relevant information? On the other hand, social media becomes popular and pervasive in disseminating information, with the sheer number of information sources, the reliability of an information source can vary dramatically, from reputable to dubious, to untrustworthy, thus arises the *information credibility* problem [17]. Without spending time verifying source credibility, how can we find reliable information? The investigation of trust helps discover an effective approach to addressing the information overload and credibility problems.

This book provides an overview of characteristics and aspects of trust from a computational perspective. Trust representations are essential for trust computing and detailed first in Chapter 2. Various types of trust prediction are discussed in Chapter 3. Trust relations in social media are often extremely sparse. Trust prediction can help answer questions such as whom should we trust, and whom shouldn't we trust. The trust-data sparsity problem also limits the extent to which trust can be applied in social media and can be addressed by trust prediction. Trust-aware recommender systems are presented in Chapter 4 as an illustrative example to demonstrate how to apply trust and help to improve their performance. Distrust is introduced in Chapter 5. As a conceptual counterpart of trust, distrust could be as important as trust and ignoring distrust could lead to the overestimate of the effect of trust. As the need for trust research becomes apparent, we present recent advances for each computational task of trust. In this chapter, we further discuss some research directions that expand the boundary of trust computing in social media. Among four computational tasks of trust, representing trust has been extensively studied and recent trends in representing trust focus on enriching representations to capture sophisticated properties of trust. For example, the dynamic multi-dimensional representation [134] is developed to capture the properties of context dependent and dynamics. In the following, we concentrate our discussion on predicting trust, applying trust, and incorporating distrust.

6.1 FUTURE DIRECTIONS IN PREDICTING TRUST

Attack-resistant Trust Metrics   In social media, users are distributed worldwide and it is very common for us to encounter strangers and some of them are bots or spammers. Trust computing can play an important role in helping us make decisions when we face uncertainty. For example, buying a product from eBay with hundreds of sellers, we depend on trustworthy scores of sellers to make purchase decisions. Trust indeed eases the decision making process. However, malicious users can also game a trust-based system. For example, malicious users form groups to accumulate reputations and promote their products [106]. Therefore, we need to design trust metrics that are robust to those ill-intended users, or attack-resistant trust metrics. Levien et al. [79] proposed bottleneck property as one feature for attack-resistant trust metrics. The bottleneck property is formally stated as: the total trust quality according to a link $u_i \rightarrow u_j$ is not significantly affected by changes of the successors of u_j. In other words, when u_i is a normal user and u_j is a malicious user, the bottleneck property suggests that manipulating the malicious user u_j has no impact on trust values inferred by attack-resistant trust metrics.

Distributed Trust Metrics   In real-world online trust systems, there are hundreds and millions of users. For example, eBay reached 157 million active users in the second quarter of 2015[1] and there are 334 million active users on Taobao in the third quarter of 2014.[2] For an online trust system with n users, the time complexity for a typical trust metric could be $O(n^2)$ or even $O(n^3)$, which is difficult, if not impossible, to finish on a single machine. Recently, frameworks such as Hadoop have been developed for distributed storage and distributed processing on computer clusters, enabling many data mining and machine learning algorithms to run in a distributed fashion, e.g., distributed matrix factorization [36]. Recent advances in distributed computing allow us to develop distrusted and scalable trust metrics for large-scale online trust systems with millions or even billions of users.

Real-time Trust Metrics   Online trust systems are highly dynamic: new content is continuously generated and new users join consecutively. Those high-velocity changes may result in swift shifting of user's collective preferences and the evolution of trust among users. For example, when people are interested in "Electronics" at time t, they trust experts in "Electronics;" while people shift their preferences to "sports" at $t + 1$, they trust experts in the facet of sports. Therefore, a trust metric should update and respond timely in order to catch users' real-time interests and trust, i.e., real-time trust metrics. Online learning updates models after the arrival of every new data point in a scalable fashion and has become an important branch of machine learning [4], providing necessary technical supports for developing real-time trust metrics.

6.2   FUTURE DIRECTIONS IN APPLYING TRUST

Weak Ties   Most existing model-based trust-aware recommender systems make use of a user's *direct* trust relations, which is conservative in estimating the diversity of users' interests. If users in the physical world only had strong ties, life would be pretty boring since strong ties often indicate strong similarities. Users can establish weak ties with others in trust networks when they are not

---

[1]http://www.statista.com/statistics/242235/number-of-ebays-total-active-users/
[2]http://www.quora.com/How-many-active-users-does-Taobao-have

directly connected. Weak ties can provide important contextual information about users' interests, and are proven to be useful in job hunting [41] and the diffusion of ideas [42].

Identifying weak ties for recommendation is an interesting direction to investigate. One possible way to find weak ties is to exploit users' geo-locations, suggested by the confounding effect: users who are geographically close are potential candidates to establish trust relations. Another possible way is to detect groups in trust networks. Connected users in trust networks form groups: there are more trust relations among users within groups than among those between groups. For example, in Figure 6.1, $\{u_1, u_2, u_3, u_{10}, u_{11}, u_{12}\}$ form a group while $\{u_1, u_4, u_5, u_{13}, u_{14}, u_{15}\}$ form another group. According to social correlation theories, similar users tend to interact more frequently than dissimilar ones, and users in the same group are likely to share similar preferences, establishing weak ties when they are not directly connected such as u_{10} and u_{11}.

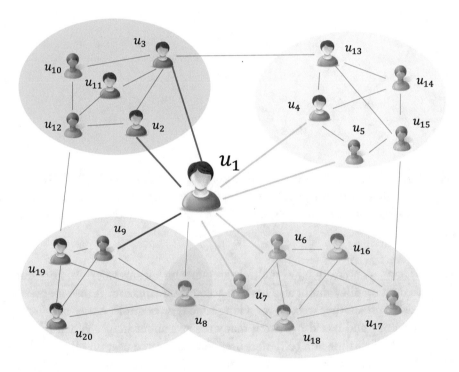

Figure 6.1: An illustration of u_1's trust network.

User Segmentation   In traditional recommender systems, ratings of users most similar to a given user are aggregated to predict a missing rating. When trust information is available, besides being similar, users are connected with trust. A user's most similar users can have little overlap with her trusted users. Therefore, users can be segmented into four groups as illustrated in Figure 6.2—I: trusted and non-similar users; II: trusted and similar users; III: non-trusted and similar users; and IV: non-trusted and non-similar users. According to the number of received ratings, items can be segmented into cold-start items and normal items. Different types of users may contribute differently for different types of items. For example, trusted users can improve the recommendation accuracy of cold-start items, while similar users are important to recommend normal items. Therefore, investigating the relationships between users and items can deepen our understanding of the role of trust networks in improving recommendation performance.

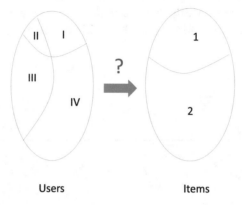

Figure 6.2: User segmentation for trust-aware recommendation, where "I," "II," "III," and "IV" denote trusted and non-similar users, trusted and similar users, non-trusted and similar users, and non-trusted and non-similar users respectively, while "1" and "2" denote cold-start items and normal items, respectively.

Cross-media Data   A user often has multiple accounts on various websites. For example, a user who has an account on eBay might also have an account on Amazon. A new user on one website might have existed on another website for a long time. For example, a user has already specified her interests on eBay and has also written many reviews about items. When the user registers for Amazon for the first time as a cold-start user, data about the user on eBay can help Amazon solve the cold-start problem and accurately recommend items to the user. Integrating information including trust networks from multiple websites can help trust-aware recommender systems and provide an efficient and effective way to solve the cold-start or data sparsity problem. The first difficulty of integrating data is to connect corresponding users across websites and there is recent work proposed to tackle this mapping problem [108, 162, 163]. The study of the mapping problem makes integration of cross-media data for trust-aware recommendation possible and brings about new opportunities for trust-aware recommender systems.

6.3   FUTURE DIRECTIONS IN INCORPORATING DISTRUST

Incorporating distrust in trust computing is still in its burgeoning development with great potential for further exploration [127]. Below we present some promising research directions.

Evaluation without Ground Truth   Assessing algorithms in Chapter 5 about incorporating distrust usually need datasets with ground truth. However, more often than not, distrust is not explicitly available in social media. A chief challenge of evaluation is how to verify the correctness of predicted distrust when distrust relations are invisible. We could take a multi-pronged approach to the evaluation challenges. Traditionally, training and test datasets are used in evaluation; in such as a case, we say there is ground truth. When ground truth is not available, user studies are conducted (e.g., employing Amazon Mechanical Turks). In Xiang et al. [150], a user study is performed to verify the performance of predicting strong and weak ties on Facebook. In essence, this method relies on a group of recruited subjects who donate their data but withhold distrust information and then compare predicted distrust against their withheld distrust. Various approaches are introduced in Zafarani and Liu [164] to evaluate social media research on datasets without ground truth and some of them can be borrowed in the study of incorporating distrust in trust computing.

Distrust in More Trust Computing Applications   Trust has been widely applied in various social media applications such as recommendation, sentiment analysis, and spammer detection. In Chapter 5, we discuss algorithms about incorporating distrust in trust-aware recommender systems and empirical evaluation demonstrates that distrust can significantly improve the recommendation performance. The encouraging progress not only validates the importance of distrust but also suggests that distrust should be taken into account in more trust applications. The success of distrust prediction and applying distrust in trust-aware recommender systems opens the door for many new trust computing applications.

Learning Representations for Trust/Distrust Networks   Trust networks are a type of unsigned networks while trust/distrust networks are signed networks. Learning representations for networks, also known as network embedding, is to learn low-dimensional vector representations for nodes of a given network, which can advance many tasks in network analysis such as link prediction and community detection [140]. The vast majority of existing embedding algorithms are designed for unsigned networks. The availability of negative links in signed networks suggests that the fundamental principles that explain the formation of links for unsigned and signed networks can be substantially different. For example, homophily and social influence for unsigned networks may be applicable differently to signed networks. Therefore, signed network embedding cannot be carried out by simply extending embedding algorithms for unsigned social networks. To learn representations for signed networks, we need: (1) an objective function for signed network embedding that differs from that for unsigned network embedding; and (2) a corresponding representation learning algorithm to optimize the objective function. Social theories are developed by social scientists to explain social phenomena in signed social networks and they provide fundamental understandings about signed social networks, which could pave the way for us to develop objective functions for signed network embedding. Meanwhile, deep learning techniques provide powerful tools for representation learning which have enhanced various domains such as speech recognition, natural language processing and computer vision [52]. It would be of great interest to see if combining social theories with deep learning algorithms could help tackle the problem of learning representations for trust/distrust networks.

Bibliography

[1] A. Abdul-Rahman and S. Hailes. Supporting trust in virtual communities. In *System Sciences, 2000. Proceedings of the 33rd Annual Hawaii International Conference on*, pages 9–pp. IEEE, 2000. DOI: 10.1109/HICSS.2000.926814. 22

[2] G. Adomavicius and A. Tuzhilin. Toward the next generation of recommender systems: A survey of the state-of-the-art and possible extensions. *Knowledge and Data Engineering, IEEE Transactions on*, 17(6):734–749, 2005. DOI: 10.1109/TKDE.2005.99. 51, 56

[3] P. Agrawal, V. K. Garg, and R. Narayanam. Link label prediction in signed social networks. In *Proceedings of the Twenty-Third International Joint Conference on Artificial Intelligence*, pages 2591–2597. AAAI Press, 2013. 85

[4] T. Anderson. *The Theory and Practice of Online Learning*. Athabasca University Press, 2008. 94

[5] D. Artz and Y. Gil. A survey of trust in computer science and the semantic web. *Web Semantics: Science, Services and Agents on the World Wide Web*, 5(2):58–71, 2007. DOI: 10.1016/j.websem.2007.03.002. 1

[6] C.-m. Au Yeung and T. Iwata. Strength of social influence in trust networks in product review sites. In *Proceedings of the Fourth ACM International Conference on Web Search and Data Mining*, pages 495–504. ACM, 2011. DOI: 10.1145/1935826.1935899. 18

[7] R. Baeza-Yates and B. Ribeiro-Neto. *Modern Information Retrieval*, volume 463. ACM press New York., 1999. 53

[8] B. Barber. *The logic and limits of trust*, volume 96. Rutgers University Press New Brunswick, NJ, 1983. 2

[9] N. J. Belkin and W. B. Croft. Information filtering and information retrieval: two sides of the same coin? *Communications of the ACM*, 35(12):29–38, 1992. DOI: 10.1145/138859.138861. 53

[10] P. Borzymek and M. Sydow. Trust and distrust prediction in social network with combined graphical and review-based attributes. In *Agent and Multi-Agent Systems: Technologies and Applications*, pages 122–131. Springer, 2010. DOI: 10.1007/978-3-642-13480-7_14. 86

[11] P. Borzymek, M. Sydow, and A. Wierzbicki. Enriching trust prediction model in social network with user rating similarity. In *Computational Aspects of Social Networks, 2009. CASON'09. International Conference on*, pages 40–47. IEEE, 2009. DOI: 10.1109/CA-SoN.2009.30. 39

[12] J. S. Breese, D. Heckerman, and C. Kadie. Empirical analysis of predictive algorithms for collaborative filtering. In *Proceedings of the Fourteenth Conference on Uncertainty in Artificial Intelligence*, pages 43–52. Morgan Kaufmann Publishers Inc., 1998. 53, 55

[13] G. Cai, J. Tang, and Y. Wen. Trust prediction with temporal dynamics. In *Web-Age Information Management*, pages 681–686. Springer, 2014. DOI: 10.1007/978-3-319-08010-9_72. 47

[14] D. Cartwright and T. C. Gleason. The number of paths and cycles in a digraph. *Psychometrika*, 31(2):179–199, 1966. DOI: 10.1007/BF02289506. 77

[15] D. Cartwright and F. Harary. Structural balance: a generalization of heider's theory. *Psychological Review*, 63(5):277, 1956. DOI: 10.1037/h0046049. 77

[16] C. Castelfranchi and R. Falcone. Towards a theory of delegation for agent-based systems. *Robotics and Autonomous Systems*, 24(3):141–157, 1998. DOI: 10.1016/S0921-8890(98)00028-1. 25

[17] C. Castillo, M. Mendoza, and B. Poblete. Information credibility on twitter. In *Proceedings of the 20th International Conference on World Wide Web*, pages 675–684. ACM, 2011. DOI: 10.1145/1963405.1963500. 93

[18] Y. Cen, R. Gu, and Y. Ji. Sign inference for dynamic signed networks via dictionary learning. *Journal of Applied Mathematics*, 2013, 2013. DOI: 10.1155/2013/708581. 85

[19] C. C. Chen, Y.-H. Wan, M.-C. Chung, and Y.-C. Sun. An effective recommendation method for cold start new users using trust and distrust networks. *Information Sciences*, 224:19–36, 2013. DOI: 10.1016/j.ins.2012.10.037. 86

[20] K.-Y. Chiang, C.-J. Hsieh, N. Natarajan, A. Tewari, and I. S. Dhillon. Prediction and clustering in signed networks: A local to global perspective. *arXiv preprint arXiv:1302.5145*, 2013. 91

[21] K.-Y. Chiang, N. Natarajan, A. Tewari, and I. S. Dhillon. Exploiting longer cycles for link prediction in signed networks. In *Proceedings of the 20th ACM International Conference on Information and Knowledge Management*, pages 1157–1162. ACM, 2011. DOI: 10.1145/2063576.2063742. 85

[22] J. Cho. The mechanism of trust and distrust formation and their relational outcomes. *Journal of Retailing*, 82(1):25–35, 2006. DOI: 10.1016/j.jretai.2005.11.002. 72, 86

[23] P. Cofta. Distrust. In *ICEC*. ACM, 2006. DOI: 10.1145/1151454.1151498. 72

[24] D. Cohn and H. Chang. Learning to probabilistically identify authoritative documents. In *ICML*, pages 167–174. Citeseer, 2000. 80

[25] J. S. Coleman. Social capital in the creation of human capital. *American Journal of Sociology*, pages S95–S120, 1988. DOI: 10.1086/228943. 74

[26] M. Cygan, M. Pilipczuk, M. Pilipczuk, and J. O. Wojtaszczyk. Sitting closer to friends than enemies, revisited. In *Mathematical Foundations of Computer Science 2012*, pages 296–307. Springer, 2012. DOI: 10.1007/978-3-642-32589-2_28. 88

[27] J. A. Davis. Clustering and structural balance in graphs. *Human Relations*, 1967. DOI: 10.1177/001872676702000206. 77, 85

[28] M. De Cock and P. P. Da Silva. A many valued representation and propagation of trust and distrust. In *Fuzzy Logic and Applications*, pages 114–120. Springer, 2006. DOI: 10.1007/11676935_14. 84

[29] C. De Kerchove and P. Van Dooren. The pagetrust algorithm: How to rank web pages when negative links are allowed? In *SDM*, pages 346–352. SIAM, 2008. DOI: 10.1137/1.9781611972788.31. 81

[30] M. Deutsch. Trust and suspicion. *Journal of Conflict Resolution*, pages 265–279, 1958. DOI: 10.1177/002200275800200401. 2

[31] P. Doreian and A. Mrvar. A partitioning approach to structural balance. *Social Networks*, 18(2):149–168, 1996. DOI: 10.1016/0378-8733(95)00259-6. 83

[32] T. DuBois, J. Golbeck, and A. Srinivasan. Predicting trust and distrust in social networks. In *Privacy, Security, Risk and Trust (passat), 2011 IEEE Third International Conference on and 2011 IEEE Third International Conference on Social Computing (Socialcom)*, pages 418–424. IEEE, 2011. DOI: 10.1109/PASSAT. 86

[33] D. Dunlavy, T. Kolda, and E. Acar. Temporal link prediction using matrix and tensor factorizations. *ACM Transactions on Knowledge Discovery from Data (TKDD)*, 5(2):10, 2011. DOI: 10.1145/1921632.1921636. 61

[34] Y. Fang and L. Si. Matrix co-factorization for recommendation with rich side information and implicit feedback. In *Proceedings of the 2nd International Workshop on Information Heterogeneity and Fusion in Recommender Systems*, pages 65–69. ACM, 2011. DOI: 10.1145/2039320.2039330. 55

[35] R. Forsati, M. Mahdavi, M. Shamsfard, and M. Sarwat. Matrix factorization with explicit trust and distrust side information for improved social recommendation. *ACM Transactions on Information Systems (TOIS)*, 32(4):17, 2014. DOI: 10.1145/2641564. 87, 88, 89

[36] R. Gemulla, E. Nijkamp, P. J. Haas, and Y. Sismanis. Large-scale matrix factorization with distributed stochastic gradient descent. In *Proceedings of the 17th ACM SIGKDD International Conference on Knowledge Discovery and Data Mining*, pages 69–77. ACM, 2011. DOI: 10.1145/2020408.2020426. 94

[37] J. Golbeck. *Generating Predictive Movie Recommendations from Trust in Social Networks.* Springer, 2006. DOI: 10.1007/11755593_8. 59

[38] J. Golbeck. *Computing with social trust.* Springer Science & Business Media, 2008. DOI: 10.1007/978-1-84800-356-9. 1, 74

[39] J. Golbeck, J. Hendler, et al. Filmtrust: Movie recommendations using trust in web-based social networks. In *Proceedings of the IEEE Consumer Communications and Networking Conference*, volume 96, pages 282–286, 2006. DOI: 10.1109/CCNC.2006.1593032. 41

[40] J. A. Golbeck. Computing and applying trust in web-based social networks. 2005. 73, 74

[41] M. Granovetter. The strength of weak ties. *American Journal of Sociology*, 78(6):1360–1380, May 1973. DOI: 10.1086/225469. 95

[42] M. Granovetter. The strength of weak ties: A network theory revisited. *Sociological Theory*, 1(1):201–233, 1983. DOI: 10.2307/202051. 95

[43] N. Griffiths. Task delegation using experience-based multi-dimensional trust. In *Proceedings of the Fourth International Joint Conference on Autonomous Agents and Multiagent Systems*, pages 489–496. ACM, 2005. DOI: 10.1145/1082473.1082548. 23, 25

[44] R. Guha, R. Kumar, P. Raghavan, and A. Tomkins. Propagation of trust and distrust. In *Proceedings of the 13th International Conference on World Wide Web*, pages 403–412. ACM, 2004. DOI: 10.1145/988672.988727. 39, 40, 71, 75, 77, 78, 84, 89

[45] I. Guy, M. Jacovi, E. Shahar, N. Meshulam, V. Soroka, and S. Farrell. Harvesting with sonar: the value of aggregating social network information. In *Proceedings of the SIGCHI Conference on Human Factors in Computing Systems*, pages 1017–1026. ACM, 2008. DOI: 10.1145/1357054.1357212. 58

[46] C.-W. Hang, Y. Wang, and M. P. Singh. Operators for propagating trust and their evaluation in social networks. In *Proceedings of The 8th International Conference on Autonomous Agents and Multiagent Systems–Volume 2*, pages 1025–1032. International Foundation for Autonomous Agents and Multiagent Systems, 2009. DOI: 10.1145/1558109.1558155. 43

[47] F. Harary. On the notion of balance of a signed graph. *The Michigan Mathematical Journal*, 2(2):143–146, 1953. DOI: 10.1307/mmj/1028989917. 77

[48] R. Hardin. *Distrust: Manifestations and management.* Russell Sage Foundation, 2004. 72, 91

[49] T. H. Haveliwala. Topic-sensitive pagerank. In *Proceedings of the 11th International Conference on World Wide Web*, pages 517–526. ACM, 2002. DOI: 10.1145/511446.511513. 34, 80

[50] F. Heider. Attitudes and cognitive organization. *The Journal of Psychology*, 21(1):107–112, 1946. DOI: 10.1080/00223980.1946.9917275. 77

[51] N. M. Henley, R. B. Horsfall, and C. B. De Soto. Goodness of figure and social structure. *Psychological Review*, 76(2):194, 1969. DOI: 10.1037/h0027358. 77

[52] G. E. Hinton, S. Osindero, and Y.-W. Teh. A fast learning algorithm for deep belief nets. *Neural Computation*, 18(7):1527–1554, 2006. DOI: 10.1162/neco.2006.18.7.1527. 98

[53] L. T. Hosmer. Trust: The connecting link between organizational theory and philosophical ethics. *Academy of Management Review*, 20(2):379–403, 1995. DOI: 10.5465/AMR.1995.9507312923. 3

[54] Y. P. Hou. Bounds for the least laplacian eigenvalue of a signed graph. *Acta Mathematica Sinica*, 21(4):955–960, 2005. DOI: 10.1007/s10114-004-0437-9. 83

[55] C.-J. Hsieh, K.-Y. Chiang, and I. S. Dhillon. Low rank modeling of signed networks. In *Proceedings of the 18th ACM SIGKDD International Conference on Knowledge Discovery and Data Mining*, pages 507–515. ACM, 2012. DOI: 10.1145/2339530.2339612. 85

[56] J. Huang, F. Nie, H. Huang, Y. Lei, and C. Ding. Social trust prediction using rank-k matrix recovery. In *Proceedings of the Twenty-Third International Joint Conference on Artificial Intelligence*, pages 2647–2653. AAAI Press, 2013. 42

[57] Z. Huang, D. Zeng, and H. Chen. A link analysis approach to recommendation under sparse data. In *Proc. 2004 Americas Conf. Information Systems*, 2004. 55

[58] M. Jamali and M. Ester. Trustwalker: a random walk model for combining trust-based and item-based recommendation. In *Proceedings of the 15th ACM SIGKDD International Conference on Knowledge Discovery and Data Mining*, pages 397–406. ACM, 2009. DOI: 10.1145/1557019.1557067. 60

[59] M. Jamali and M. Ester. A matrix factorization technique with trust propagation for recommendation in social networks. In *Proceedings of the Fourth ACM Conference on Recommender Systems*, pages 135–142. ACM, 2010. DOI: 10.1145/1864708.1864736. 64

[60] A. Javari and M. Jalili. Cluster-based collaborative filtering for sign prediction in social networks with positive and negative links. *ACM Transactions on Intelligent Systems and Technology (TIST)*, 5(2):24, 2014. DOI: 10.1145/2501977. 83, 84

[61] A. Josang, E. Gray, and M. Kinateder. Analysing topologies of transitive trust. In *Proc. of the 1st Workshop on Formal Aspects in Security and Trust (FAST2003)*, 2003. 72

[62] A. Jøsang, R. Ismail, and C. Boyd. A survey of trust and reputation systems for online service provision. *Decision Support Systems*, 43(2):618–644, 2007. DOI: 10.1016/j.dss.2005.05.019. 1, 5, 29, 34

[63] A. Jsang and R. Ismail. The beta reputation system. In *Proceedings of the 15th Bled Electronic Commerce Conference*, volume 5, pages 2502–2511, 2002. 21

[64] S. D. Kamvar, M. T. Schlosser, and H. Garcia-Molina. The eigentrust algorithm for reputation management in p2p networks. In *Proceedings of the 12th International Conference on World Wide Web*, pages 640–651. ACM, 2003. DOI: 10.1145/775152.775242. 33, 51

[65] G. Karypis. Evaluation of item-based top-n recommendation algorithms. In *Proceedings of the Tenth International Conference on Information and knowledge Management*, pages 247–254. ACM, 2001. DOI: 10.1145/502585.502627. 53

[66] Khaled M. Khan and Qutaibah Malluhi, "Establishing Trust in Cloud Computing," *IT Professional*, vol. 12, no. 5, pages 20–27, 2010. 10

[67] D. J. Kim, Y. I. Song, S. B. Braynov, and H. R. Rao. A multidimensional trust formation model in b-to-c e-commerce: a conceptual framework and content analyses of academia/practitioner perspectives. *Decision Support Systems*, 40(2):143–165, 2005. DOI: 10.1016/j.dss.2004.01.006. 25

[68] S. Knapskog. A metric for trusted systems. In *Proceedings of the 21st National Security Conference*, pages 16–29. Citeseer, 1998. 84

[69] Y. Koren. Factorization meets the neighborhood: a multifaceted collaborative filtering model. In *Proceeding of the 14th ACM SIGKDD International Conference on Knowledge Discovery and Data Mining*, pages 426–434. ACM, 2008. DOI: 10.1145/1401890.1401944. 53, 55, 67

[70] N. Korovaiko and A. Thomo. Trust prediction from user-item ratings. *Social Network Analysis and Mining*, 3(3):749–759, 2013. DOI: 10.1007/s13278-013-0122-z. 36

[71] M. Kosfeld, M. Heinrichs, P. J. Zak, U. Fischbacher, and E. Fehr. Oxytocin increases trust in humans. *Nature*, 435(7042):673–676, 2005. DOI: 10.1038/nature03701. 3

[72] B. Kosko. Fuzzy cognitive maps. *International Journal of Man-machine Studies*, 24(1):65–75, 1986. DOI: 10.1016/S0020-7373(86)80040-2. 22

[73] D. Kreps and R. Wilson. Reputation and imperfect information. *Journal of Economic Theory*, 27, page 253–79, 1982. 3

[74] J. Kunegis, A. Lommatzsch, and C. Bauckhage. The slashdot zoo: mining a social network with negative edges. In *Proceedings of the 18th International Conference on World Wide Web*, pages 741–750. ACM, 2009. DOI: 10.1145/1526709.1526809. 81

[75] S. M. Lee and M. Mellat-Parast. The formation of initial trust in the strategic supply chain partnership. *International Journal of Management and Enterprise Development*, 7(1):28–43, 2009. DOI: 10.1504/IJMED.2009.025264. 3

[76] M. Lesani and S. Bagheri. Applying and inferring fuzzy trust in semantic web social networks. In *Canadian Semantic Web*, pages 23–43. Springer, 2006. DOI: 10.1007/978-0-387-34347-1_3. 22

[77] J. Leskovec, D. Huttenlocher, and J. Kleinberg. Predicting positive and negative links in online social networks. In *Proceedings of the 19th International Conference on World Wide Web*, pages 641–650. ACM, 2010. DOI: 10.1145/1772690.1772756. 76, 77, 85

[78] J. Leskovec, D. Huttenlocher, and J. Kleinberg. Signed networks in social media. In *Proceedings of the SIGCHI Conference on Human Factors in Computing Systems*, pages 1361–1370. ACM, 2010. DOI: 10.1145/1753326.1753532. 77, 78, 79

[79] R. Levien. Attack-resistant trust metrics. In *Computing with Social Trust*, pages 121–132. Springer, 2009. DOI: 10.1007/978-1-84800-356-9_5. 94

[80] R. J. Lewicki, D. J. McAllister, and R. J. Bies. Trust and distrust: New relationships and realities. *Academy of Management Review*, 23(3):438–458, 1998. DOI: 10.2307/259288. 2, 72

[81] J. D. Lewis and A. Weigert. Trust as a social reality. *Social Forces*, 63(4):967–985, 1985. DOI: 10.1093/sf/63.4.967. 3

[82] Y. Li, J. Hu, C. Zhai, and Y. Chen. Improving one-class collaborative filtering by incorporating rich user information. In *Proceedings of the 19th ACM International Conference on Information and Knowledge Management*, pages 959–968. ACM, 2010. DOI: 10.1145/1871437.1871559. 55

[83] R. N. Lichtenwalter, J. T. Lussier, and N. V. Chawla. New perspectives and methods in link prediction. In *Proceedings of the 16th ACM SIGKDD International Conference on Knowledge Discovery and Data Mining*, pages 243–252. ACM, 2010. DOI: 10.1145/1835804.1835837. 85

[84] H. Liu, E.-P. Lim, H. W. Lauw, M.-T. Le, A. Sun, J. Srivastava, and Y. Kim. Predicting trusts among users of online communities: an epinions case study. In *Proceedings of the 9th ACM Conference on Electronic Commerce*, pages 310–319. ACM, 2008. DOI: 10.1145/1386790.1386838. 35, 36

[85] E. Lorenz. Trust, contract and economic cooperation. *Cambridge Journal of Economics*, 23(3):301–315, 1999. DOI: 10.1093/cje/23.3.301. 3

[86] N. Luhmann. *Trust and Power*. Wiley Chichester, 1979. 72

[87] H. Ma, I. King, and M. R. Lyu. Learning to recommend with social trust ensemble. In *Proceedings of the 32nd International ACM SIGIR Conference on Research and Development in Information Retrieval*, pages 203–210. ACM, 2009. DOI: 10.1145/1571941.1571978. 63

[88] H. Ma, M. R. Lyu, and I. King. Learning to recommend with trust and distrust relationships. In *Proceedings of the Third ACM Conference on Recommender Systems*, pages 189–196. ACM, 2009. DOI: 10.1145/1639714.1639746. 87, 88

[89] H. Ma, H. Yang, M. Lyu, and I. King. Sorec: social recommendation using probabilistic matrix factorization. In *Proceeding of the 17th ACM Conference on Information and Knowledge Management*, pages 931–940. ACM, 2008. DOI: 10.1145/1458082.1458205. 62

[90] H. Ma, D. Zhou, C. Liu, M. Lyu, and I. King. Recommender systems with social regularization. In *Proceedings of the Fourth ACM International Conference on Web Search and Data Mining*, pages 287–296. ACM, 2011. DOI: 10.1145/1935826.1935877. 64

[91] H. Ma, D. Zhou, C. Liu, M. R. Lyu, and I. King. Recommender systems with social regularization. In *Proceedings of the Fourth ACM International Conference on Web Search and Data Mining*, pages 287–296. ACM, 2011. DOI: 10.1145/1935826.1935877. 88

[92] N. Ma, E.-P. Lim, V.-A. Nguyen, A. Sun, and H. Liu. Trust relationship prediction using online product review data. In *Proceedings of the 1st ACM International Workshop on Complex Networks Meet Information & Knowledge Management*, pages 47–54. ACM, 2009. DOI: 10.1145/1651274.1651284. 36

[93] P. V. Marsden and N. E. Friedkin. Network studies of social influence. *Sociological Methods & Research*, 22(1):127–151, 1993. DOI: 10.1177/0049124193022001006. 16

[94] S. Marsh and M. R. Dibben. Trust, untrust, distrust and mistrust–an exploration of the dark (er) side. In *Trust Management*, pages 17–33. Springer, 2005. DOI: 10.1007/11429760_2. 72

[95] P. Massa. A survey of trust use and modeling in real online systems. *Trust E-services: Technologies, Practices and Challenges. Idea Group Inc.*, pages 51–83, 2007. 1, 4, 5

[96] P. Massa and P. Avesani. Controversial users demand local trust metrics: An experimental study on epinions. com community. In *Proceedings of the National Conference on Artificial Intelligence*, volume 20, page 121. Menlo Park, CA; Cambridge, MA; London; AAAI Press; MIT Press; 1999, 2005. 41

[97] P. Massa and P. Avesani. Trust-aware recommender systems. In *Proceedings of the 2007 ACM Conference on Recommender Systems*, pages 17–24. ACM, 2007. DOI: 10.1145/1297231.1297235. 51, 65

[98] P. Massa and P. Avesani. Trust-aware recommender systems. In *Proceedings of the 2007 ACM Conference on Recommender Systems*, pages 17–24. ACM, 2007. DOI: 10.1145/1297231.1297235. 59

[99] R. C. Mayer, J. H. Davis, and F. D. Schoorman. An integrative model of organizational trust. *Academy of Management Review*, 20(3):709–734, 1995. DOI: 10.2307/258792. 3

[100] D. H. McKnight and N. L. Chervany. Trust and distrust definitions: One bite at a time. In *Trust in Cyber-societies*, pages 27–54. Springer, 2001. DOI: 10.1007/3-540-45547-7_3. 2, 4

[101] D. H. McKnight and V. Choudhury. Distrust and trust in b2c e-commerce: Do they differ? In *ICEC*, pages 482–491. ACM, 2006. DOI: 10.1145/1151454.1151527. 72

[102] M. McPherson, L. Smith-Lovin, and J. M. Cook. Birds of a feather: Homophily in social networks. *Annual Review of Sociology*, pages 415–444, 2001. DOI: 10.1146/annurev.soc.27.1.415. 15

[103] A. Mishra and A. Bhattacharya. Finding the bias and prestige of nodes in networks based on trust scores. In *Proceedings of the 20th International Conference on World Wide Web*, pages 567–576. ACM, 2011. DOI: 10.1145/1963405.1963485. 82

[104] R. Morgan and S. Hunt. The Commitment-Trust Theory of Relationship Marketing. *The Journal of Marketing*, 58(3):20–-38, July 1994. DOI: 10.2307/1252308 3

[105] L. Mui, M. Mohtashemi, and A. Halberstadt. A computational model of trust and reputation. In *System Sciences, 2002. HICSS. Proceedings of the 35th Annual Hawaii International Conference on*, pages 2431–2439. IEEE, 2002. DOI: 10.1109/HICSS.2002.994181. 4

[106] A. Mukherjee, B. Liu, J. Wang, N. Glance, and N. Jindal. Detecting group review spam. In *Proceedings of the 20th International Conference Companion on World Wide Web*, pages 93–94. ACM, 2011. DOI: 10.1145/1963192.1963240. 94

[107] U. Nalluri. Utility of distrust in online recommender systems. *Capstone Project Report*, 2014. 86, 87

[108] A. Narayanan and V. Shmatikov. De-anonymizing Social Networks. In *Security and Privacy, 2009 30th IEEE Symposium on*, pages 173–187. IEEE, 2009. DOI: 10.1109/SP.2009.22. 96

[109] V.-A. Nguyen, E.-P. Lim, J. Jiang, and A. Sun. To trust or not to trust? predicting online trusts using trust antecedent framework. In *Data Mining, 2009. ICDM'09. Ninth IEEE International Conference on*, pages 896–901. IEEE, 2009. DOI: 10.1109/ICDM.2009.115. 36

[110] L. Page, S. Brin, R. Motwani, and T. Winograd. The Pagerank Citation Ranking: Bringing Order to the Web. 1999. 33, 71

[111] A. Papaoikonomou, M. Kardara, K. Tserpes, and D. Varvarigou. Edge sign prediction in social networks via frequent subgraph discovery. *IEEE Internet Computing*, 2014. DOI: 10.1109/MIC.2014.82. 86

[112] A. Patidar, V. Agarwal, and K. Bharadwaj. Predicting friends and foes in signed networks using inductive inference and social balance theory. In *Proceedings of the 2012 International Conference on Advances in Social Networks Analysis and Mining (ASONAM 2012)*, pages 384–388. IEEE Computer Society, 2012. DOI: 10.1109/ASONAM.2012.69. 86

[113] Milan Petkovic and Willem Jonker. *Security, Privacy and Trust in Modern Data Management (Data-Centric Systems and Applications)*. Springer-Verlag New York, Inc., Secaucus, NJ, USA, 2007. 10

[114] S. Raghavan, S. Gunasekar, and J. Ghosh. Review quality aware collaborative filtering. In *Proceedings of the Sixth ACM Conference on Recommender Systems*, pages 123–130. ACM, 2012. DOI: 10.1145/2365952.2365978. 55

[115] S. Reece, A. Rogers, S. Roberts, and N. R. Jennings. Rumours and reputation: Evaluating multi-dimensional trust within a decentralised reputation system. In *Proceedings of the 6th International Joint Conference on Autonomous Agents and Multiagent Systems*, page 165. ACM, 2007. DOI: 10.1145/1329125.1329326. 26

[116] J. B. Rotter. Interpersonal trust, trustworthiness, and gullibility. *American Psychologist*, 35(1):1, 1980. DOI: 10.1037/0003-066X.35.1.1. 2

[117] J. Sabater and C. Sierra. Reputation and social network analysis in multi-agent systems, *Proceedings of the First Int. Joint Conference on Autonomous Agents and Multiagent Systems (AAMAS)*, July, 2002. 34

[118] R. Salakhutdinov and A. Mnih. Probabilistic matrix factorization. *Advances in Neural Information Processing Systems*, 20:1257–1264, 2008. 55

[119] B. Sarwar, G. Karypis, J. Konstan, and J. Riedl. Item-based collaborative filtering recommendation algorithms. In *Proceedings of the 10th International Conference on World Wide Web*, pages 285–295. ACM, 2001. DOI: 10.1145/371920.372071. 51, 53

[120] B. R. Schlenker, B. Helm, and J. T. Tedeschi. The effects of personality and situational variables on behavioral trust. *Journal of Personality and Social Psychology*, 25(3):419, 1973. DOI: 10.1037/h0034088. 2

[121] D. Seno and B. Lukas. The equity effect of product endorsement by celebrities: A conceptual framework from a co-branding perspective. *European Journal of Marketing*, 2007. DOI: 10.1108/03090560710718148. 69

[122] M. Shahriari and M. Jalili. Ranking nodes in signed social networks. *Social Network Analysis and Mining*, 4(1):1–12, 2014. DOI: 10.1007/s13278-014-0172-x. 81

[123] Y. L. Sun, W. Yu, Z. Han, and K. Liu. Information theoretic framework of trust modeling and evaluation for ad hoc networks. *Selected Areas in Communications, IEEE Journal on*, 24(2):305–317, 2006. DOI: 10.1109/JSAC.2005.861389. 41

[124] P. Symeonidis and N. Mantas. Spectral clustering for link prediction in social networks with positive and negative links. *Social Network Analysis and Mining*, 3(4):1433–1447, 2013. DOI: 10.1007/s13278-013-0128-6. 83

[125] P. Symeonidis and E. Tiakas. Transitive node similarity: predicting and recommending links in signed social networks. *World Wide Web*, pages 1–34, 2013. DOI: 10.1007/s11280-013-0228-2. 83, 84

[126] M. Szell, R. Lambiotte, and S. Thurner. Multirelational organization of large-scale social networks in an online world. *Proceedings of the National Academy of Sciences*, 107(31):13636–13641, 2010. DOI: 10.1073/pnas.1004008107. 74, 76, 78

[127] J. Tang. *Computing Distrust in Social Media*. Ph.D. thesis, Arizona State University, 2015. 10, 26, 97

[128] J. Tang, C. Aggarwal, and H. Liu. Recommendation with signed social networks. In *Submitted to The 37th Annual ACM SIGIR Conference*, 2015. 87, 88, 89

[129] J. Tang, S. Chang, C. Aggarwal, and H. Liu. Negative link prediction in social media. In *ACM International Conference on Web Search and Data Mining*, 2015. DOI: 10.1145/2684822.2685295. 89, 91, 92

[130] J. Tang, Y. Chang, and H. Liu. Mining social media with social theories: A survey. *SIGKDD Explorations*, 2013. DOI: 10.1145/2641190.2641195. 77

[131] J. Tang, H. Gao, X. Hu, and H. Liu. Context-aware review helpfulness rating prediction. In *RecSys*, 2013. DOI: 10.1145/2507157.2507183. 57

[132] J. Tang, H. Gao, X. Hu, and H. Liu. Exploiting homophily effect for trust prediction. In *Proceedings of the Sixth ACM International Conference on Web Search and Data Mining*, pages 53–62. ACM, 2013. DOI: 10.1145/2433396.2433405. 18, 41, 48, 58, 69, 75

[133] J. Tang, H. Gao, and H. Liu. mTrust: discerning multi-faceted trust in a connected world. In *Proceedings of the Fifth ACM International Conference on Web Search and Data Mining*, pages 93–102. ACM, 2012. DOI: 10.1145/2124295.2124309. 15, 18, 23, 24, 26, 43, 46, 63, 66, 70

[134] J. Tang, H. Gao, H. Liu, and A. Das Sarma. eTrust: Understanding trust evolution in an online world. In *Proceedings of the 18th ACM SIGKDD International Conference on Knowledge Discovery and Data Mining*, pages 253–261. ACM, 2012. DOI: 10.1145/2339530.2339574. 19, 26, 43, 66, 93

[135] J. Tang, X. Hu, Y. Chang, and H. Liu. Predictability of distrust with interaction data. In *ACM International Conference on Information and Knowledge Management*, 2014. DOI: 10.1145/2661829.2661988. 66, 85, 89, 90, 91

[136] J. Tang, X. Hu, H. Gao, and H. Liu. Exploiting local and global social context for recommendation. In *Proceedings of the Twenty-Third International Joint Conference on Artificial Intelligence*, pages 2712–2718. AAAI Press, 2013. 55, 62

[137] J. Tang, X. Hu, and H. Liu. Social recommendation: a review. *Social Network Analysis and Mining*, 3(4):1113–1133, 2013. DOI: 10.1007/s13278-013-0141-9. 61

[138] J. Tang, X. Hu, and H. Liu. Is distrust the negation of trust? the value of distrust in social media. In *ACM Hypertext Conference*, 2014. DOI: 10.1145/2631775.2631793. 13, 71, 73, 74, 75, 90

[139] J. Tang and H. Liu. Trust in social computing. In *Proceedings of the Companion Publication of the 23rd International Conference on World Wide Web Companion*, pages 207–208. International World Wide Web Conferences Steering Committee, 2014. DOI: 10.1145/2567948.2577265. 1, 28, 72, 85

[140] L. Tang and H. Liu. Community detection and mining in social media. *Synthesis Lectures on Data Mining and Knowledge Discovery*, 2(1):1–137, 2010. DOI: 10.2200/S00298ED1V01Y201009DMK003. 97

[141] E. Terzi and M. Winkler. A spectral algorithm for computing social balance. In *Algorithms and Models for the Web Graph*, pages 1–13. Springer, 2011. DOI: 10.1007/978-3-642-21286-4_1. 77

[142] V. Traag, Y. Nesterov, and P. Van Dooren. Exponential ranking: Taking into account negative links. *Social Informatics*, pages 192–202, 2010. DOI: 10.1007/978-3-642-16567-2_14. 71, 81

[143] L. H. Ungar and D. P. Foster. Clustering methods for collaborative filtering. In *AAAI Workshop on Recommendation Systems*, number 1, 1998. 55

[144] P. Victor, C. Cornelis, M. De Cock, and P. Pinheiro da Silva. Towards a provenance-preserving trust model in agent networks. In *WWW2006 Conference Proceedings, Special Interest Tracks, Posters and Workshops*, 2006. 84

[145] P. Victor, C. Cornelis, M. De Cock, and A. Teredesai. Trust-and distrust-based recommendations for controversial reviews. In *Web Science Conference (WebSci'09: Society On-Line)*, number 161, 2009. DOI: 10.1109/MIS.2011.22. 86, 87, 89

[146] P. Victor, M. De Cock, and C. Cornelis. Trust and recommendations. In *Recommender Systems Handbook*, pages 645–675. Springer, 2011. DOI: 10.1007/978-0-387-85820-3_20. 59

[147] P. Victor, N. Verbiest, C. Cornelis, and M. D. Cock. Enhancing the trust-based recommendation process with explicit distrust. *ACM Transactions on the Web (TWEB)*, 7(2):6, 2013. DOI: 10.1145/2460383.2460385. 86, 87

[148] Y. Wang, X. Wang, J. Tang, W. Zuo, and G. Cai. Modeling status theory in trust prediction. In *Twenty-Ninth AAAI Conference on Artificial Intelligence*, 2015. 48

[149] R. Xiang, J. Neville, and M. Rogati. Modeling relationship strength in online social networks. In *Proceedings of the 19th International Conference on World Wide Web*, 2010. DOI: 10.1145/1772690.1772790. 61

[150] R. Xiang, J. Neville, and M. Rogati. Modeling relationship strength in online social networks. In *Proceedings of the 19th International Conference on World Wide Web*, pages 981–990. ACM, 2010. DOI: 10.1145/1772690.1772790. 97

[151] W. Xing and A. Ghorbani. Weighted pagerank algorithm. In *Communication Networks and Services Research, 2004. Proceedings. Second Annual Conference on*, pages 305–314. IEEE, 2004. DOI: 10.1109/DNSR.2004.1344743. 34

[152] L. Xiong and L. Liu. Peertrust: Supporting reputation-based trust for peer-to-peer electronic communities. *Knowledge and Data Engineering, IEEE Transactions on*, 16(7):843–857, 2004. DOI: 10.1109/TKDE.2004.1318566. 33

[153] Z. Yan and S. Holtmanns. Trust modeling and management: from social trust to digital trust. *IGI Global*, pages 290–323, 2008. 19

[154] S.-H. Yang, A. J. Smola, B. Long, H. Zha, and Y. Chang. Friend or frenemy?: predicting signed ties in social networks. In *Proceedings of the 35th International ACM SIGIR Conference on Research and Development in Information Retrieval*, pages 555–564. ACM, 2012. DOI: 10.1145/2348283.2348359. 78, 89, 90, 91

[155] X. Yang, H. Steck, and Y. Liu. Circle-based recommendation in online social networks. In *Proceedings of the 18th ACM SIGKDD International Conference on Knowledge Discovery and Data Mining*, pages 1267–1275. ACM, 2012. DOI: 10.1145/2339530.2339728. 70

[156] Y. Yao, H. Tong, X. Yan, F. Xu, and J. Lu. Matri: a multi-aspect and transitive trust inference model. In *Proceedings of the 22nd International Conference on World Wide Web*, pages 1467–1476. International World Wide Web Conferences Steering Committee, 2013. 42

[157] H. Yildirim and M. S. Krishnamoorthy. A random walk method for alleviating the sparsity problem in collaborative filtering. In *Proceedings of the 2008 ACM Conference on Recommender Systems*, pages 131–138. ACM, 2008. DOI: 10.1145/1454008.1454031. 55

[158] B. Yu and M.P. Singh. An evidential model of distributed reputation management, *Proceedings of the First Int. Joint Conference on Autonomous Agents and Multiagent Systems (AAMAS)*, ACM, 2002 (July). 34

[159] X. Yu and J. Xie. Learning interactions for social prediction in large-scale networks. In *Proceedings of the 23rd ACM International Conference on Conference on Information and Knowledge Management*, pages 161–170. ACM, 2014. DOI: 10.1145/2661829.2662056. 91

[160] X. Yu and J. Q. Xie. Modeling mutual influence between social actions and social ties. 2014. 91

[161] R. Zafarani, M. A. Abbasi, and H. Liu. *Social Media Mining: An Introduction*. Cambridge University Press, 2014. 9

[162] R. Zafarani and H. Liu. Connecting corresponding identities across communities. In *Proceedings of the 3rd International Conference on Weblogs and Social Media (ICWSM09)*, 2009. 96

[163] R. Zafarani and H. Liu. Connecting users across social media sites: a behavioral-modeling approach. In *Proceedings of the 19th ACM SIGKDD International Conference on Knowledge Discovery and Data Mining*, pages 41–49. ACM, 2013. DOI: 10.1145/2487575.2487648. 96

[164] R. Zafarani and H. Liu. Evaluation without ground truth in social media research. *Communications of the ACM*, 58(6):54–60, 2015. DOI: 10.1145/2666680. 97

[165] T. Zhang, H. Jiang, Z. Bao, and Y. Zhang. Characterization and edge sign prediction in signed networks. *Journal of Industrial and Intelligent Information*, Vol. 1(1), 2013. 86

[166] X. Zhang, L. Cui, and Y. Wang. Commtrust: computing multi-dimensional trust by mining e-commerce feedback comments. *Knowledge and Data Engineering, IEEE Transactions on*, 26(7):1631–1643, 2014. DOI: 10.1109/TKDE.2013.177. 25

[167] R. Zhou and K. Hwang.   Powertrust: A robust and scalable reputation system for trusted peer-to-peer computing. *Parallel and Distributed Systems, IEEE Transactions on*, 18(4):460–473, 2007. DOI: 10.1109/TPDS.2007.1021. 33

[168] C.-N. Ziegler and J. Golbeck. Investigating interactions of trust and interest similarity. *Decision Support Systems*, 43(2):460–475, 2007. DOI: 10.1016/j.dss.2006.11.003. 17, 38, 74

[169] C.-N. Ziegler and G. Lausen. Propagation models for trust and distrust in social networks. *Information Systems Frontiers*, 7(4-5):337–358, 2005. DOI: 10.1007/s10796-005-4807-3. 41, 84

[170] K. Zolfaghar and A. Aghaie. Mining trust and distrust relationships in social web applications. In *Intelligent Computer Communication and Processing (ICCP), 2010 IEEE International Conference on*, pages 73–80. IEEE, 2010. DOI: 10.1109/ICCP.2010.5606460. 81

[171] K. Zolfaghar and A. Aghaie. A syntactical approach for interpersonal trust prediction in social web applications: Combining contextual and structural data. *Knowledge-Based Systems*, 26:93–102, 2012. DOI: 10.1016/j.knosys.2010.10.007. 37

[172] L. G. Zucker. Production of trust: Institutional sources of economic structure, 1840–1920. *Research in Organizational Behavior*, 1986. 2

Authors' Biographies

JILIANG TANG

Jiliang Tang is a research scientist at Yahoo Labs. He received his Ph.D. in computer science at Arizona State University in 2014, and B.S./M.S. from Beijing Institute of Technology in 2008 and 2010, respectively. His research interests include trust/distrust computing, feature selection, social computing, data mining, and machine learning. He was awarded the Runner Up of SIGKDD Dissertation Award 2015, Dean's Dissertation Award 2015, Outstanding Graduating Computer Science Ph.D. Student 2015, the 2014 ASU President's Award for Innovation, Best Paper Shortlist in WSDM13, the 3rd Place Dedicated Task 2 Next Location Prediction of Nokia Mobile Data Challenge 2012, University Graduate Fellowship, and various Student Travel Awards and Scholarships. He co-presented three tutorials in KDD2014, WWW2014, and Recsys2014, and has published innovative works in highly ranked journals and top conference proceedings such as ACM Computing Survey, IEEE TKDE, ACM TKDD, DMKD, ACM SIGKDD, SIGIR, WWW, WSDM, SDM, ICDM, IJCAI, AAAI, and CIKM.

HUAN LIU

Huan Liu is a professor of computer science and engineering at Arizona State University. He obtained his Ph.D. in computer science at University of Southern California and B.Eng. in computer science and electrical engineering at Shanghai JiaoTong University. Before he joined ASU, he worked at Telecom Australia Research Labs and was on the faculty at National University of Singapore. He was recognized for excellence in teaching and research in computer science and engineering at Arizona State University. His research interests are in data mining, machine learning, social computing, and artificial intelligence, investigating problems that arise in many real-world, data-intensive applications with high-dimensional data of disparate forms such as social media. His well-cited publications include books, book chapters, encyclopedia entries, as well as conference and journal papers. He serves on journal editorial boards and numerous conference program committees, and is a founding organizer of the International Conference Series on Social Computing, Behavioral-Cultural Modeling, and Prediction (`http://sbp.asu.edu/`). He is an IEEE Fellow. Updated information can be found at `http://www.public.asu.edu/~huanliu`.